W9-BVD-267

Taste of Home

THE new
slow cooker
the best recipes for today's one-pot meals

Taste of Home
B O O K S

REIMAN MEDIA GROUP, INC. • GREENDALE, WISCONSIN

A TASTE OF HOME/READER'S DIGEST BOOK

© 2007 Reiman Media Group, Inc.
5400 S. 60th St., Greendale WI 53129
All rights reserved.

Taste of Home and Reader's Digest are registered trademarks of The Reader's Digest Association, Inc.

Editor	Jennifer Olski
Associate Editor	Jean Steiner
Art Director	Julie Wagner
Cover Design	Edwin Robles, Jr.
Proofreader	Linne Bruskewitz
Editorial Assistant	Barb Czysz
Recipe Testing and Editing	Taste of Home Test Kitchen
Food Photography	Reiman Photo Studio
Senior Editor, Retail Books	Jennifer Olski
Vice President/Executive Editor, Books	Heidi Reuter Lloyd
Creative Director	Ardyth Cope
Senior Vice President, Editor in Chief	Catherine Cassidy
President	Barbara Newton
Founder	Roy Reiman

Pictured on front cover:
Hobo Meatball Stew (recipe on p. 42)

International Standard Book Number (10): 0-89821-583-8
International Standard Book Number (13): 978-0-89821-583-0

Library of Congress Control Number: 2006939045

For other Taste of Home books and products, visit www.tasteofhome.com.
For more Reader's Digest products and information, visit
www.rd.com (in the United States)
www.rd.ca (in Canada).

Printed in China.
3 5 7 9 10 8 6 4 2

table of contents

THE NEW SLOW COOKER

THE new slow cooker

With 225 slow-cooked, satisfying appetizers, beverages, entrees, sides and desserts, you'll be on the fast track to fixing mouth-watering meals!

GOOD COOKS KNOW THAT THE SECRET TO SUCCESS FOR FUSS-FREE FAMILY MEALS starts with a slow cooker. Whether you're a long-time fan of the slow cooker or someone who's just discovered that you don't have to be a slave to the stove when it comes to home-cooked meals, you can enjoy 225 of the tastiest recipes for weekday meals, special occasion get-togethers and bring-a-dish gatherings.

All the recipes in this book were shared by cooks like you and tested by experienced home economists in the Taste of Home Test Kitchen. So you can rest assured that every dish you fix is a tried-and-true success.

In this big book, you'll discover helpful hints to make meal preparation easier and more enjoyable. You'll also find practical cooking shortcuts and time-saving kitchen tips and much more.

So turn to *The New Slow Cooker* for delectable dining inspiration and convenience any day of the week...and savor fresh new tastes from your favorite kitchen stand-by.

Difference Between A Crock-Pot® And a Slow Cooker

The original slow cooker, called a Crock-Pot, was introduced in 1971 by Rival®. The term "slow cooker" and the name Crock-Pot are frequently used interchangeably when referring to this appliance.

The most popular slow cookers have heat coils circling a crockery insert. With this type, the heat surrounds the food to help it cook evenly. These models have two heat settings: "high" (equal to 300°F) and "low" (equal to 200°F).

Other types of slow cookers have heat coils on the bottom and have an adjustable thermostat.

All the recipes in this cookbook refer to cooking on either "high" or "low" for a certain amount of time.

When a time range is provided, this accounts for variables such as thickness of meat, how full the slow cooker is, temperature of the food going into the cooker, etc.

As you become more familiar with your slow cooker, you'll be better able to judge which end of the range to use for cooking food.

A handy attribute of slow cookers is that if you can't get home at exactly the time the food should be done, it generally doesn't hurt to leave the slow cooker cooking on low for an extra hour.

Selecting the Right Slow Cooker Size

Slow cookers come in a range of sizes, from 1 quart to 6 quarts. It's important to use the right size for the amount of food you're making.

To cook properly and safely, manufacturers and the USDA recommend slow cookers be filled at least half full but no more than two-thirds full. Check the chart at left to find the proper size slow cooker for you.

In general, to serve a dip from a buffet, the smallest slow cookers are ideal. To entertain or cook for a potluck dinner, the larger cookers work best.

Many slow cookers have a removable stoneware insert. That handy feature also allows you to assemble the food the night before, when it's convenient for you. Uncooked meats should be stored separately from other ingredients and added when you're ready to cook.

Cover and store the insert in the refrigerator. Then in the morning, you can just put in the insert, turn on the cooker and go.

Note: Don't preheat the base unit. An insert that has been in the refrigerator overnight should always be put into a cold base unit. Stoneware is sensitive to dramatic temperature changes and cracking or breakage could occur with preheating.

Another option, especially for recipes that require additional preparation like browning meat, is to assemble your recipe in the evening, put everything in the slow cooker and turn it on. Let it cook overnight while you sleep.

In the morning, when the recipe has cooked for the required amount of time, store your finished dish in the refrigerator and reheat it in the microwave at dinnertime.

Slow Cooker Size Recommendation

1 person household	1 to 1-1/2 quarts
2 people	2 to 3-1/2 quarts
3 or 4 people	3-1/2 to 4-1/2 quarts
4 or 5 people	4-1/2 to 5 quarts
6 or more people	5 to 6 quarts

Preparing Foods for The Slow Cooker

Meats. For enhanced flavor and appearance, meat may be browned before going into the slow cooker, but it's not necessary. If you decide not to brown the meat, you may want to add color when serving by sprinkling on some chopped parsley or shredded cheese. Garnishes such as fresh herbs and lemon wedges can also help.

Vegetables. Vegetables, especially root vegetables like carrots and potatoes, tend to cook slower than meat. Place these vegetables on the bottom and around the sides of the slow cooker and put meat on top of the vegetables. Add tender vegetables like peas and zucchini, or those you'd prefer to be crisp-tender, during the last 15 to 60 minutes of cooking.

Dairy. Most milk-based products tend to break down during slow cooking. If possible, add items like milk, sour cream, cream cheese or cream during the last hour of cooking. Cheeses don't generally hold up over extended periods of cooking, so they should be added near the end of cooking—or use processed cheeses instead.

Seasonings. Whole herbs and spices are better than the crushed forms in the slow cooker. The whole berry or leaf is firmer and stands up better over long cooking times. They'll be at their peak at serving time. Add fresh herbs just before the end of cooking.

Beans. Dried beans can be tricky to work with in the slow cooker. Minerals in the water and variations in voltage affect different types of beans in different ways. As a result, dried beans should always be soaked before adding to a slow cooker recipe. Here's how:

Place beans in a Dutch oven or soup kettle; add water to cover by 2 inches. Bring to a boil; boil for 2 minutes. Remove from the heat; cover and let stand for 1 hour. Drain and rinse beans, discarding liquid.

Note: Lentils and split peas do not need to be soaked. After dried beans are completely cooked, they can be combined with sugar and/or acidic foods, such as tomato sauce. Sugar and acid have a hardening effect on beans and will prevent them from becoming tender. An alternative is to use canned beans that have been rinsed and drained.

Pasta. If added to a slow cooker when dry, pasta becomes very sticky. Partially cook pasta until it's almost tender but not completely cooked before adding. Or, boil pasta until it's completely tender and add it at the end of cooking just to heat it through and blend it with the other ingredients.

Fish. Fish is very tender and turns into flakes if slow cooked for long periods. Add fish during the last 20 minutes of cooking.

slow cooker basics

• No peeking! Refrain from lifting the lid while the slow cooker is cooking unless you're instructed in a recipe to stir or add ingredients. The loss of steam can mean an additional 15 to 30 minutes of cooking time each time you lift the lid.

• Be sure the lid is seated properly—not tilted or askew. The steam during cooking creates a seal.

• Remove food from the slow cooker within 1 hour after it's finished cooking. Promptly refrigerate leftovers.

• Slow cooking may take longer at higher altitudes.

Converting Recipes For the Slow Cooker

Almost any recipe that bakes in the oven or simmers on the stovetop can be converted for the slow cooker. Here are some guidelines:

Using this book or the manufacturer's instruction booklet, locate a recipe similar to the one you want to convert. Use it as a guide. Note the quantity and size of meat and vegetable pieces, heat setting, cooking time and amount of liquid.

Note: Since there is no evaporation, foods tend to water down. If your recipe calls for 6 to 8 cups of water, you might want to start with 5 cups. Conversely, recipes should include some liquid. If a recipe doesn't include liquid, add 1/2 cup of water or broth.

In general, 1 hour of simmering on the range or baking at 350°F in the oven is equal to 8-10 hours on low or 4-5 hours on high in a slow cooker. Check the chart above.

Thickeners such as flour, cornstarch and tomato paste are used to give texture to foods cooked in the slow cooker.

Before converting recipes, check manufacturer's guidelines for your particular slow cooker.

Conventional Cooking Time	Slow Cooker Cooking Time
15 to 30 min.	Low: 4 to 6 hours High: 1-1/2 to 2 hours
35 to 45 min.	Low: 6 to 8 hours High: 3 to 4 hours
50 min. or more	Low: 8 to 10 hours High: 4 to 6 hours

helpful foil handles

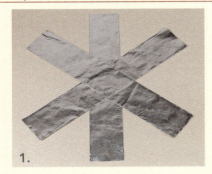

1.

2.

3.

Meat loaves and some layered dishes are easier to get out of the slow cooker using foil handles. Here's how:

1. Cut three 20- x 3-inch strips of heavy-duty aluminum foil. Crisscross the strips so they resemble the spokes of a wheel.

2. Place the meat loaf in the center of the strips, and pull them up and bend the edges to form handles.

3. Grasp the foil handles to lift the loaf and lower it into the slow cooker. Leave the foil in while cooking so you can easily lift the meat out to serve.

Note: For a layered dish, place the strips in the cooker and up the sides before putting in the food. Leave them in. Once the food is cooked, pull the strips together as a handle to neatly remove the food in one piece.

Cleaning Your Slow Cooker

Removable stoneware inserts make cleanup a breeze. Be sure to cool the insert before adding water for cleaning to avoid cracking.

Wash the insert in the dishwasher or in warm, soapy water. Avoid using abrasive cleansers since they may scratch the stoneware.

To remove mineral stains on a crockery insert, fill the cooker with hot water and 1 cup white vinegar; cover. Turn heat control to high for 2 hours.

Then empty. When cool, wash with hot, sudsy water and a cloth or sponge. Rinse well and dry with a towel.

To remove water marks from a highly glazed crockery insert, rub the surface with vegetable oil and allow to stand for 2 hours before washing with hot sudsy water.

Do not immerse the metal base unit. Clean it with a damp sponge.

Special Uses

Don't forget your slow cooker when you go camping, provided electricity is available. It's a handy appliance when space is limited and you want "set-it-and-forget-it" meals.

Reheating foods in a slow cooker is not recommended. Cooked food can be brought to steaming on the stovetop or in the microwave and then put into a preheated slow cooker to keep hot for serving.

Use a slow cooker on a buffet table to keep soup, stew or mashed potatoes hot.

check your slow cooker operation

Did you inherit a used slow cooker or find one at a garage sale and want to see if it's working properly?

To be considered safe, a slow cooker must be able to cook slow enough so that it can be left unattended, yet it must be fast enough to keep the food at a safe temperature. Here's how to check:

1. Fill the slow cooker with 2 quarts of lukewarm water.

2. Heat on low with the lid covered for 8 hours.

3. Using a thermometer, check the temperature of the water quickly since the temperature can drop quite a bit once the lid is removed.

4. The temperature should be at 185°F. If it's too hot, your meal cooked for 8 hours would likely be overdone. If the temperature is below 185°, it could be the cooker does not heat food to an adequate temperature to avoid the growth of harmful bacteria.

appetizers & beverages

18

30

Whether you're planning a family feast or a casual get-together for friends, set up your slow cooker to handle the appetizers and beverages. While you focus on the final details of your meal, these savory starters, like Hot Chili Dip (p. 18) or Hot Cranberry Punch (p. 30), can simmer and finish cooking.

These favorite dips, salsas, fondues, finger foods and drinks call for everyday ingredients and little prep. So it's easy and affordable to add an extra course to a weeknight dinner or a Saturday celebration!

championship bean dip

COOK TIME: 2 HOURS

- 1 can (16 ounces) refried beans
- 1 cup picante sauce
- 1 cup (4 ounces) shredded Monterey Jack cheese
- 1 cup (4 ounces) shredded cheddar cheese
- 3/4 cup sour cream
- 1 package (3 ounces) cream cheese, softened
- 1 tablespoon chili powder
- 1/4 teaspoon ground cumin

Tortilla chips and salsa

In a bowl, combine the first eight ingredients; transfer to a slow cooker. Cover and cook on high for 2 hours or until heated through, stirring once or twice. Serve with tortilla chips and salsa.

YIELD: 4 1/2 CUPS.

Wendi Wavrin Law, Omaha, Nebraska

My friends and neighbors expect me to bring this irresistible dip to every gathering. When I arrive, they ask, "You brought your bean dip, didn't you?" If there are any leftovers, we use them to make bean and cheese burritos the next day.

peppered meatballs

COOK TIME: 2 HOURS

- $^1\!/_2$ cup sour cream
- 2 teaspoons grated Parmesan *or* Romano cheese
- 2 to 3 teaspoons pepper
- 1 teaspoon salt
- 1 teaspoon dry bread crumbs
- $^1\!/_2$ teaspoon garlic powder
- $1^1\!/_2$ pounds ground beef

SAUCE:

- 1 cup (8 ounces) sour cream
- 1 can (10-3/4 ounces) condensed cream of mushroom soup, undiluted
- 2 teaspoons dill weed
- $^1\!/_2$ teaspoon sugar
- $^1\!/_2$ teaspoon pepper
- $^1\!/_4$ teaspoon garlic powder

1 In a bowl, combine sour cream and Parmesan cheese. Add pepper, salt, bread crumbs and garlic powder. Crumble meat over mixture and mix well. Shape into 1-in. balls. Place in a greased 15-in. x 10-in. x 1-in. baking pan. Bake at 350° for 20-25 minutes or until no longer pink.

2 Transfer meatballs to a slow cooker. Combine the sauce ingredients; pour over meatballs. Cover and cook on high for 2 hours or until heated through.

YIELD: $1^1\!/_2$ DOZEN (2 CUPS SAUCE).

Darla Schroeder, Stanley, North Dakota

Plenty of ground pepper gives these saucy meatballs their tantalizing zest. They're so hearty, I sometimes serve them over noodles as a main course.

pizza dip

Sara Nowacki, Franklin, Wisconsin

Everybody loves this simple dip. If you have any left over, spoon it on toasted English muffins for a great open-faced sandwich.

COOK TIME: 1½ TO 2 HOURS

- 2 packages (8 ounces *each*) cream cheese, cubed
- 1 can (14 ounces) pizza sauce
- 1 package (8 ounces) sliced pepperoni, chopped
- 1 can (3.8 ounces) chopped ripe olives, drained
- 2 cups (8 ounces) shredded part-skim mozzarella cheese

Bagel chips *or* garlic toast

Place the cream cheese in a 3-qt. slow cooker. Combine the pizza sauce, pepperoni and olives; pour over cream cheese. Top with mozzarella cheese. Cover and cook on low for 1½ to 2 hours or until cheese is melted. Stir; serve warm with bagel chips or garlic toast.

YIELD: 5½ CUPS.

slow-cooked smokies

COOK TIME: 6 TO 7 HOURS

- 1 package (1 pound) miniature smoked sausage links
- 1 bottle (28 ounces) barbecue sauce
- 1¼ cups water
- 3 tablespoons Worcestershire sauce
- 3 tablespoons steak sauce
- ½ teaspoon pepper

In a slow cooker, combine all ingredients; mix well. Cover and cook on low for 6-7 hours. Serve with a slotted spoon.

YIELD: 8 SERVINGS.

Sundra Hauck, Bogalusa, Louisiana

I like to include these little smokies smothered in barbecue sauce on all my appetizer buffets since they're popular with both children and adults.

cheddar fondue

COOK TIME: SERVE IN SLOW COOKER

- ¼ cup butter
- ¼ cup all-purpose flour
- ½ teaspoon salt, optional
- ¼ teaspoon pepper
- ¼ teaspoon ground mustard
- ¼ teaspoon Worcestershire sauce
- 1½ cups milk
- 2 cups (8 ounces) shredded cheddar cheese

Bread cubes, ham cubes, bite-size sausage *and/or* broccoli florets

1 In a saucepan, melt butter; stir in flour, salt if desired, pepper, mustard and Worcestershire sauce until smooth. Gradually add milk. Bring to a boil; cook and stir for 2 minutes or until thickened. Reduce heat. Add the cheese; cook and stir until melted.

2 Transfer to a slow cooker; cover and keep warm on low. Serve with bread, ham, sausage and/or broccoli.

YIELD: 2½ CUPS.

Norene Wright, Manilla, Indiana

This cheesy blend, sparked with mustard and Worcestershire sauce, is yummy to snack on.

slow-cooked salsa

Toni Menard, Lompoc, California

I love the fresh taste of homemade salsa, but as a working mother, I don't have much time to make it. So I came up with this delicious, slow-cooked version that practically makes itself!

COOK TIME: 2½ TO 3 HOURS

- 10 plum tomatoes, cored
- 2 garlic cloves
- 1 small onion, cut into wedges
- 2 jalapeno peppers
- ¼ cup fresh cilantro
- ½ teaspoon salt

Tortilla chips

1 Cut a small slit in two tomatoes; insert a garlic clove into each slit. Place tomatoes and onion in a slow cooker. Cut stem off jalapenos; remove seeds if a milder salsa is desired. Place jalapenos in slow cooker. Cover and cook on high for 2½ to 3 hours or until vegetables are softened (some may brown); cool.

2 In a blender or food processor, combine tomato mixture, cilantro and salt; cover and process until smooth. Serve with tortilla chips.

YIELD: ABOUT 2 CUPS.

EDITOR'S NOTE: When cutting or seeding hot peppers, use rubber or plastic gloves to protect your hands. Avoid touching your face.

hot chili dip

COOK TIME: 1 TO 2 HOURS

- 1 jar (24 ounces) salsa
- 1 can (15 ounces) chili with beans
- 2 cans (2¼ ounces *each*) sliced ripe olives, drained
- 12 ounces process cheese (Velveeta), cubed

Tortilla chips

In a small slow cooker, combine the salsa, chili and olives. Stir in cheese. Cover and cook on low for 1-2 hours or until the cheese is melted, stirring halfway through. Serve with tortilla chips.

YIELD: ABOUT 2 CUPS.

Nikki Rosati, Franksville, Wisconsin

I first made this zippy dip for my husband's birthday party.
Many of our family members and friends asked for the recipe.

cheesy pizza fondue

COOK TIME: SERVE IN SLOW COOKER

- ½ pound ground beef
- 1 medium onion, chopped
- 2 cans (15 ounces *each*) pizza sauce
- 1½ teaspoons dried basil *or* oregano
- ¼ teaspoon garlic powder
- 2½ cups (10 ounces) shredded sharp cheddar cheese
- 1 cup (4 ounces) shredded part-skim mozzarella cheese

Breadsticks

1 In a heavy saucepan, cook beef and onion over medium heat until meat is no longer pink; drain. Stir in the pizza sauce, basil and garlic powder; mix well.

2 Reduce heat to low. Add cheeses; stir until melted. Transfer to a slow cooker or fondue pot and keep warm over low heat. Serve with breadsticks.

YIELD: ABOUT 5 CUPS.

Julie Barwick, Mansfield, Ohio

While I was growing up, I would sit for hours reading cookbooks from cover to cover. I've carried that love of cooking with me through the years. I found this recipe when we lived in Wisconsin.

marinated chicken wings

COOK TIME: 3½ TO 4 HOURS

20 whole chicken wings
    (about 4 pounds)

 2 cups soy sauce

½ cup white wine *or* chicken broth

½ cup vegetable oil

 2 to 3 garlic cloves, minced

 2 tablespoons sugar

 2 teaspoons ground ginger

1 Cut chicken wings into three sections; discard wing tips. Place wings in a large resealable heavy-duty plastic bag or 13-in. x 9-in. x 2-in. baking dish. In a bowl, combine remaining ingredients; mix well. Pour half of the sauce over chicken; turn to coat. Seal or cover the chicken and remaining sauce; refrigerate overnight.

2 Drain chicken, discarding the marinade. Place the chicken in a 5-qt. slow cooker; top with the reserved sauce. Cover and cook on low for 3½ to 4 hours or until chicken juices run clear. Transfer wings to a serving dish; discard cooking juices.

YIELD: 18-20 SERVINGS.

EDITOR'S NOTE: 4 pounds of uncooked chicken wing sections may be substituted for the whole wings. Omit the first step of the recipe.

Janie Botting, Sultan, Washington

I've made these nicely flavored chicken wings many times for get-togethers. They're so moist and tender…and a nice alternative to the spicy wings made with hot pepper sauce.

hot crab dip

COOK TIME: 3 TO 4 HOURS

- ½ cup milk
- ⅓ cup salsa
- 3 packages (8 ounces *each*) cream cheese, cubed
- 2 packages (8 ounces *each*) imitation crabmeat, flaked
- 1 cup thinly sliced green onions
- 1 can (4 ounces) chopped green chilies

Assorted crackers

1 Combine milk and salsa. Transfer to a slow cooker coated with nonstick cooking spray. Stir in cream cheese, crab, onions and chilies.

2 Cover and cook on low for 3-4 hours, stirring every 30 minutes. Serve with crackers.

YIELD: ABOUT 5 CUPS.

Teri Rasey-Bolf, Cadillac, Michigan

As a busy mother and grandmother, I appreciate recipes like this that are easy to assemble. The rich, creamy dip is an appetizer that always goes over well during the holidays.

all-day meatballs

Cathy Ryan, Red Wing, Minnesota

For those who love to entertain but don't want last-minute fuss, these hearty meatballs are perfect. They're easy to make, tender and have a tangy sauce.

COOK TIME: 6 TO 8 HOURS

- 1 cup milk
- ¾ cup quick-cooking oats
- 3 tablespoons finely chopped onion
- 1½ teaspoons salt
- 1½ pounds ground beef
- 1 cup ketchup
- ½ cup water
- 3 tablespoons vinegar
- 2 tablespoons sugar

1 In a bowl, combine the first four ingredients. Crumble beef over the mixture and mix well. Shape into 1-in. balls. Place in a slow cooker.

2 In a bowl, combine the ketchup, water, vinegar and sugar; mix well. Pour over meatballs. Cover and cook on low for 6-8 hours or until the meat is no longer pink.

YIELD: 6 SERVINGS.

slow cooker party mix

COOK TIME: 3 HOURS

4 cups Wheat Chex

4 cups Cheerios

3 cups pretzel sticks

1 can (12 ounces) salted peanuts

¼ cup butter, melted

2 to 3 tablespoons grated Parmesan cheese

1 teaspoon celery salt

½ to ¾ teaspoon seasoned salt

1 In a 5-qt. slow cooker, combine cereals, pretzels and peanuts. Combine butter, Parmesan cheese, celery salt and seasoned salt; drizzle over cereal mixture and mix well.

2 Cover and cook on low for up to 3 hours, stirring every 30 minutes. Serve warm or at room temperature.

YIELD: ABOUT 3 QUARTS.

Dana Hughes, Gresham, Oregon

This mildly seasoned snack mix is always a party favorite. The munchable mixture is very satisfying, especially when it's served warm from a slow cooker, which makes it extra special.

paddy's reuben dip

COOK TIME: 2 HOURS

4 packages (2½ ounces *each*) deli corned beef, finely chopped

1 package (8 ounces) cream cheese, cubed

1 can (8 ounces) sauerkraut, rinsed and drained

1 cup (8 ounces) sour cream

1 cup (4 ounces) shredded Swiss cheese

Rye bread *or* crackers

In a mini slow cooker, combine the first five ingredients. Cover and cook on low for 2 hours or until cheese is melted; stir until blended. Serve warm with bread or crackers.

YIELD: ABOUT 4 CUPS.

Mary Jane Kimmes, Hastings, Minnesota

This slow-cooked spread tastes just like a Reuben sandwich. Even when I double the recipe, I end up with an empty dish.

creamy chipped beef fondue

Beth Fox, Lawrence, Kansas

My mother often served fondue during the holidays and I've since followed in that tradition. It's nice to offer a hearty appetizer like this creamy treat that requires very little work.

COOK TIME: SERVE IN SLOW COOKER

1⅓ to 1½ cups milk

2 packages (8 ounces *each*) cream cheese, cubed

1 package (2½ ounces) thinly sliced dried beef, chopped

¼ cup chopped green onions

2 teaspoons ground mustard

1 loaf (1 pound) French bread, cubed

1 In a saucepan, heat milk and cream cheese over medium heat; stir until smooth. Stir in beef, onions and mustard; heat through.

2 Transfer to a fondue pot or slow cooker; keep warm. Serve with bread cubes.

YIELD: ABOUT 4 CUPS.

spiced coffee

COOK TIME: 2 TO 3 HOURS

8 cups brewed coffee

1/3 cup sugar

1/4 cup chocolate syrup

1/2 teaspoon anise extract

4 cinnamon sticks (3 inches), halved

1 1/2 teaspoons whole cloves

Additional cinnamon sticks, optional

1 In a slow cooker, combine the first four ingredients; mix well. Place cinnamon sticks and cloves in a double thickness of cheesecloth; bring up corners of cloth and tie with string to form a bag. Add to slow cooker.

2 Cover and cook on low for 2-3 hours. Discard spice bag. Ladle coffee into mugs; garnish each with a cinnamon stick if desired.

YIELD: 8 CUPS.

Joanne Holt, Bowling Green, Ohio

Even those who usually don't drink coffee will find this spiced blend with a hint of chocolate appealing. I keep a big batch simmering when I host a brunch or open house.

peachy spiced cider

COOK TIME: 4 TO 6 HOURS

4 cans (5½ ounces *each*) peach nectar

2 cups apple juice

¼ to ½ teaspoon ground ginger

¼ teaspoon ground cinnamon

¼ teaspoon ground nutmeg

4 fresh orange slices (¼ inch thick), halved

Combine the first five ingredients in a slow cooker. Top with the orange slices. Cover and cook on low for 4-6 hours or until heated through. Stir before serving.

YIELD: ABOUT 1 QUART.

Rose Harman, Hays, Kansas

It's nice to welcome guests with the inviting aroma of this warm beverage. I served this spiced cider at a Christmas cookie exchange and received many compliments. Everyone seemed to enjoy the subtle peach flavor.

slow cooker cider

COOK TIME: 2 TO 5 HOURS

2 cinnamon sticks (4 inches)

1 teaspoon whole cloves

1 teaspoon whole allspice

2 quarts apple cider

½ cup packed brown sugar

1 medium orange, sliced

1 Place cinnamon, cloves and allspice in a double thickness of cheese-cloth; bring up the corners of cloth and tie with a string to form a bag.

2 Place cider and brown sugar in a slow cooker; stir until sugar dissolves. Add spice bag. Place orange slices on top. Cover and cook on low for 2-5 hours. Remove spice bag before serving.

YIELD: 2 QUARTS.

Alpha Wilson, Roswell, New Mexico

Family and friends feel warmly welcomed when they enjoy the aroma and flavor of this wonderful warm cider. Best of all, slow cooking means no last-minute rush.

hot cranberry punch

COOK TIME: 2 TO 3 HOURS

  8 cups hot water

1½ cups sugar

  4 cups cranberry juice

¾ cup orange juice

¼ cup lemon juice

12 whole cloves, optional

½ cup red-hot candies

1 In a 5-qt. slow cooker, combine water, sugar and juices; stir until sugar is dissolved. If desired, place cloves in a double thickness of cheese-cloth; bring up corners of cloth and tie with string to form a bag. Add spice bag and red-hots to slow cooker.

2 Cover and cook on low for 2-3 hours or until heated though. Before serving, discard spice bag and stir punch.

YIELD: 3½ QUARTS.

Laura Burgess, Ballwin, Missouri

I serve this rosy spiced beverage at parties and family gatherings during the winter. Friends like the tangy twist it gets from red-hot candies. It's a nice change from the usual hot chocolate.

spiced apricot cider

COOK TIME: 2 HOURS

  2 cans (12 ounces *each*) apricot
     nectar

  2 cups water

  ¼ cup lemon juice

  ¼ cup sugar

  2 whole cloves

  2 cinnamon sticks (3 inches)

Additional cinnamon sticks, optional

In a 3-qt. slow cooker, combine the first six ingredients. Cover and cook on low for 2 hours or until cider reaches desired temperature. Remove cloves and cinnamon sticks before serving. Garnish each cup with a cinnamon stick if desired.

YIELD: 6 SERVINGS.

Connie Cummings, Gloucester, New Jersey

You'll need just six ingredients to simmer together this hot spiced beverage. Each delicious mugful is rich with apricot flavor.

mulled grape cider

Sharon Harmon, Orange, Massachusetts

I created this recipe one year when I tried to make grape jelly and ended up with jars of grape syrup instead. Knowing that people like hot apple cider, I simmered the syrup with spices to make a beverage. My friends raved over it.

COOK TIME: 3 HOURS

- 5 pounds Concord grapes
- 8 cups water, *divided*
- 1½ cups sugar
- 8 whole cloves
- 4 cinnamon sticks (4 inches)

Dash ground nutmeg

1 In a large saucepan or Dutch oven, combine grapes and 2 cups water; bring to a boil, stirring constantly. Press through a strainer; reserve juice and discard skins and seeds. Pour juice through a double layer of cheesecloth into a slow cooker.

2 Add sugar, cloves, cinnamon sticks, nutmeg and remaining water. Heat on low for 3 hours. Discard cloves and cinnamon sticks before serving.

YIELD: 10-12 SERVINGS (2¾ QUARTS).

hot spiced punch

COOK TIME: 4 HOURS

- 1 jar (21.1 ounces) orange breakfast drink mix
- 1 jar (6 ounces) sugar-free instant lemon iced tea mix
- 2/3 cup sweetened lemonade drink mix
- 2 teaspoons ground cinnamon
- 1 teaspoon ground cloves

ADDITIONAL INGREDIENTS FOR HOT SPICED TEA:
- 1 cup boiling water

ADDITIONAL INGREDIENTS FOR HOT SPICED PUNCH:
- 2 quarts apple juice *or* cider
- 1½ cups cranberry juice
- 3 cinnamon sticks (3½ inches)

In an airtight container, combine the first five ingredients. Store in a cool dry place for up to 6 months.

YIELD: ABOUT 7½ CUPS TOTAL.

TO PREPARE TEA: Dissolve about 1 tablespoon tea mix in boiling water; stir well.

YIELD: 1 SERVING.

TO PREPARE PUNCH: In a 3-qt. slow cooker, combine the juices, ¼ to ⅓ cup tea mix and cinnamon sticks. Cover and cook on low for 4 hours.

YIELD: ABOUT 12 SERVINGS (6 OUNCES EACH).

Deb McKinney, Cedar Falls, Iowa

My family has relied on this homespun mix to make hot spiced tea and a heartwarming punch. My parents always served steaming mugs of this punch at Thanksgiving. It was everyone's favorite.

harvest apple cider

COOK TIME: 2 HOURS

- 8 whole cloves
- 4 cups apple cider
- 4 cups pineapple juice
- ½ cup water
- 1 cinnamon stick (3 inches)
- 1 individual tea bag

1 Place cloves on a double thickness of cheesecloth; bring up corners of cloth and tie with kitchen string to form a bag. Place the remaining ingredients in a 3-qt. slow cooker; add spice bag.

2 Cover and cook on low for 2 hours or until cider reaches desired temperature. Discard spice bag, cinnamon stick and tea bag before serving.

YIELD: ABOUT 2 QUARTS.

Lesley Geisel, Severna Park, Maryland
I simmer this comforting cider in my slow cooker every fall.

hot citrus cider

COOK TIME: 2 TO 4 HOURS

- 2 quarts apple cider
- 1 cup pineapple juice
- 1 cup orange juice
- 1 tablespoon brown sugar
- 1 tablespoon lemon juice
- 1/8 teaspoon salt
- 8 whole cloves
- 4 unpeeled fresh orange slices (1/4 inch thick)
- 4 cinnamon sticks (3 inches)

1 In a slow cooker, combine the first six ingredients. Push two cloves through each orange slice. Push a cinnamon stick through the center of each orange slice; add to cider mixture.

2 Cover and cook on low for 2-4 hours or until heated through. Discard oranges, cloves and cinnamon sticks. Stir cider before serving.

YIELD: 2 1/2 QUARTS.

Catherine Allan, Twin Falls, Idaho

I first tasted a steaming mug of this comforting beverage on a chilly evening. It's still a family favorite on a wintry day. We love the mix of fruit juices and subtle sweetness and spice.

hearty soups & stews

50

70

A savory bowl of home-style soup warms the spirit and satisfies hungry appetites. Choose from chunky Hearty Bean Soup (p. 50), spicy Green Chili Stew (p. 70) or any other soup, stew, chili or chowder when you're hankering for something hot and filling.

Plug in your slow cooker before you leave in the morning, toss in some fresh ingredients and then look forward to the enticing aromas later that day. Your one-pot recipe will be ready to serve and enjoy when you return home.

slow-cooked sauerkraut soup

Linda Lohr, Lititz, Pennsylvania

We live in Lancaster County, Pennsylvania, which has a rich heritage of German culture. Dishes that include sauerkraut, potatoes and sausage abound here. We enjoy this recipe on cold winter evenings, along with muffins and fruit.

COOK TIME: 5 TO 6 HOURS

- 1 medium potato, cut into ¼-inch cubes
- 1 pound smoked kielbasa, cut into ½-inch cubes
- 1 can (32 ounces) sauerkraut, rinsed and drained
- 4 cups chicken broth
- 1 can (10¾ ounces) condensed cream of mushroom soup, undiluted
- ½ pound fresh mushrooms, sliced
- 1 cup cubed cooked chicken
- 2 medium carrots, cut into ¼-inch slices
- 2 celery ribs, sliced
- 2 tablespoons vinegar
- 2 teaspoons dill weed
- ½ teaspoon pepper
- 3 to 4 bacon strips, cooked and crumbled

In a 5-qt. slow cooker, combine the first 12 ingredients. Cover and cook on high for 5-6 hours or until the vegetables are tender. Skim fat. Garnish individual servings with bacon.

YIELD: 10-12 SERVINGS (ABOUT 3 QUARTS).

easy warm bread

To warm rolls or slices of bread to go with a stew, wrap them in foil and set them in the covered cooker right on top of the hot cooked stew as you're setting the table to serve.

flavorful white chili

COOK TIME: 8 TO 9 HOURS

- 1 pound dried great northern beans, rinsed and sorted
- 4 cups chicken broth
- 2 cups chopped onions
- 3 garlic cloves, minced
- 2 teaspoons ground cumin
- 1½ teaspoons dried oregano
- 1 teaspoon ground coriander
- ⅛ teaspoon ground cloves
- ⅛ teaspoon cayenne pepper
- 1 can (4 ounces) chopped green chilies
- ½ pound boneless skinless chicken breast, grilled and cubed
- 1 teaspoon salt
- ¾ cup shredded reduced-fat Mexican cheese blend

1 Place beans in a soup kettle or Dutch oven; add water to cover by 2 in. Bring to a boil; boil for 2 minutes. Remove from the heat; cover and let stand for 1 hour. Drain and rinse beans, discarding liquid.

2 Place beans in a slow cooker. Add the broth, onions, garlic and seasonings. Cover and cook on low for 7-8 hours or until beans are almost tender. Add the chilies, chicken and salt; cover and cook for 1 hour or until the beans are tender. Serve with cheese.

YIELD: 6 SERVINGS.

Wilda Bensenhaver, Deland, Florida

For a tasty twist on conventional chili, try this low-fat version. It's packed with plenty of beans, tender grilled chicken and a zippy blend of spices.

smoked sausage soup

2 cups chopped onion

2 tablespoons butter

2 cups cubed cooked chicken

1 pound cooked smoked sausage, cut into bite-size pieces

3 cups sliced celery

3 cups sliced summer squash

2 cups chicken broth

1½ cups minced fresh parsley

1 can (8 ounces) tomato sauce

2 tablespoons cornstarch

2 tablespoons poultry seasoning

1 teaspoon dried oregano

1 teaspoon ground cumin

1 teaspoon Liquid Smoke, optional

½ teaspoon pepper

In a skillet or microwave, cook onion in butter until softened. Transfer to a 3-qt. or larger slow cooker. Add remaining ingredients, stirring to blend. Cook on high for 5-8 hours.

YIELD: 6-8 SERVINGS (2½ QUARTS).

Rachel Lyn Grasmick, Rocky Ford, Colorado

This rich soup is packed with vegetables, sausage and chicken. I guarantee it's unlike any other soup you've ever tasted.

hobo meatball stew

COOK TIME: 5 HOURS

- 1 pound ground beef
- 1½ teaspoons salt, *divided*
- ½ teaspoon pepper, *divided*
- 4 medium potatoes, peeled and cut into chunks
- 4 medium carrots, cut into chunks
- 1 large onion, cut into chunks
- ½ cup ketchup
- ½ cup water
- 1½ teaspoons cider vinegar
- ½ teaspoon dried basil
- ¾ cup frozen peas

1 In a bowl, combine beef, 1 teaspoon salt and ¼ teaspoon pepper; mix well. Shape into 1-in. balls. In a skillet over medium heat, brown meatballs on all sides; drain.

2 Place the potatoes, carrots and onion in a slow cooker; top with the meatballs. Combine the ketchup, water, vinegar, basil, and remaining salt and pepper; pour over meatballs. Cover and cook on high for 4 hours and 45 minutes. Stir in peas; cook 15 minutes longer or until the vegetables are tender.

YIELD: 4 SERVINGS.

Margery Bryan, Royal City, Washington

Basic ingredients make this hearty stew a favorite. I usually have everything on hand for this recipe, so it's simple to load up the slow cooker at noon. When I get home, dinner's ready.

spicy chicken tomato soup

COOK TIME: 4 HOURS

- 2 cans (14½ ounces *each*) chicken broth
- 3 cups cubed cooked chicken
- 2 cups frozen corn
- 1 can (10¾ ounces) tomato puree
- 1 can (10 ounces) diced tomatoes and green chilies
- 1 large onion, finely chopped
- 2 garlic cloves, minced
- 1 bay leaf
- 1 to 2 teaspoons ground cumin
- 1 teaspoon salt
- ½ to 1 teaspoon chili powder
- ⅛ teaspoon pepper
- ⅛ teaspoon cayenne pepper
- 4 white *or* yellow corn tortillas (6 inches), cut into ¼-inch strips

In a slow cooker, combine the first 13 ingredients. Cover and cook on low for 4 hours. Place the tortilla strips on an ungreased baking sheet. Bake at 375° for 5 minutes; turn. Bake 5 minutes longer. Discard bay leaf from soup. Serve with tortilla strips.

YIELD: 8 SERVINGS.

Margaret Bailey, Coffeeville, Mississippi

Cumin, chili powder and cayenne pepper give this slow-cooked soup its kick. I serve bowls of it with crunchy tortilla strips that bake in no time. Leftover soup freezes well for nights I don't feel like cooking.

barbecued beef chili

Phyllis Shyan, Elgin, Illinois

Served with bread and a side salad, this beefy chili makes a hearty meal. The recipe was inspired by two friends when we were talking about food at a potluck barbecue.

COOK TIME: 6 TO 7 HOURS

- 7 teaspoons chili powder
- 1 tablespoon garlic powder
- 2 teaspoons celery seed
- 1 teaspoon coarsely ground pepper
- ¼ to ½ teaspoon cayenne pepper
- 1 fresh beef brisket (3 to 4 pounds)
- 1 medium green pepper, chopped
- 1 small onion, chopped
- 1 bottle (12 ounces) chili sauce
- 1 cup ketchup
- ½ cup barbecue sauce
- ⅓ cup packed brown sugar
- ¼ cup cider vinegar
- ¼ cup Worcestershire sauce
- 1 teaspoon ground mustard
- 1 can (15½ ounces) hot chili beans
- 1 can (15½ ounces) great northern beans, rinsed and drained

1 Combine the first five ingredients; rub over brisket. Cut into eight pieces; place in a slow cooker. Combine green pepper, onion, chili sauce, ketchup, barbecue sauce, brown sugar, vinegar, Worcestershire sauce and mustard; pour over meat. Cover and cook on high for 5-6 hours or until meat is tender.

2 Remove meat; cool slightly. Meanwhile, skim fat from cooking juices. Shred meat with two forks; return to slow cooker. Reduce heat to low. Stir in the beans. Cover and cook for 1 hour or until heated through.

YIELD: 12 SERVINGS.

EDITOR'S NOTE: This recipe calls for a fresh beef brisket, not corned beef.

seafood chowder

COOK TIME: 4 TO 5 HOURS

- 1 can (10¾ ounces) condensed cream of potato soup, undiluted
- 1 can (10¾ ounces) condensed cream of mushroom soup, undiluted
- 2½ cups milk
- 4 medium carrots, finely chopped
- 2 medium potatoes, peeled and cut into ¼-inch cubes
- 1 large onion, finely chopped
- 2 celery ribs, finely chopped
- 1 can (6½ ounces) chopped clams, drained
- 1 can (6 ounces) medium shrimp, drained
- 4 ounces imitation crabmeat, flaked
- 5 bacon strips, cooked, crumbled

1 In a slow cooker, combine soups and milk. Stir in the vegetables. Cover and cook on low for 4-5 hours.

2 Stir in clams, shrimp and crab; cover and heat through, about 20 minutes. Garnish each serving with bacon.

YIELD: 8 SERVINGS.

Marlene Muckenhirn, Delano, Minnesota

Our family requests this creamy chowder for Christmas Eve supper.

It's an easy-to-serve and easy-to-clean-up meal between the church service and our gift exchange.

savory cheese soup

COOK TIME: 7½ TO 8½ HOURS

- 3 cans (14½ ounces *each*) chicken broth
- 1 small onion, chopped
- 1 large carrot, chopped
- 1 celery rib, chopped
- ¼ cup chopped sweet red pepper
- 2 tablespoons butter
- 1 teaspoon salt
- ½ teaspoon pepper
- ⅓ cup all-purpose flour
- ⅓ cup cold water
- 1 package (8 ounces) cream cheese, cubed and softened
- 2 cups (8 ounces) shredded cheddar cheese
- 1 can (12 ounces) beer, optional

Optional toppings: croutons, popcorn, cooked crumbled bacon, sliced green onions

1 In a slow cooker, combine the first eight ingredients. Cover and cook on low for 7-8 hours. Combine flour and water until smooth; stir into soup.

2 Cover and cook on high 30 minutes longer or until soup is thickened. Stir in cream cheese and cheddar cheese until blended. Stir in beer if desired. Cover and cook on low until heated through. Serve with desired toppings.

YIELD: 6-8 SERVINGS.

Ann Huseby, Lakeville, Minnesota

This creamy soup is great at parties. Let guests serve themselves and choose from fun garnishes such as popcorn, croutons, green onions and bacon bits.

beef barley stew

COOK TIME: 6 TO 7 HOURS

1½ pounds beef stew meat, cut into 1-inch pieces

1 medium onion, chopped

2 tablespoons vegetable oil

1 quart water

1 can (15 ounces) tomato sauce

5 medium carrots, cut into ½-inch pieces

1 celery rib, thinly sliced

2 teaspoons salt

½ teaspoon dried oregano

½ teaspoon paprika

¼ teaspoon pepper

2 cups fresh *or* frozen green beans

2 cups fresh *or* frozen corn

¾ cup medium pearl barley

1 In a skillet, brown beef and onion in oil; drain. Transfer to a 5-qt. slow cooker. Add water, tomato sauce, carrots, celery, salt, oregano, paprika and pepper.

2 Cover and cook on low for 4-5 hours. Add beans, corn and barley; cover and cook on low 2 hours longer or until barley, beef and vegetables are tender.

YIELD: 6-8 SERVINGS.

Barb Smith, Regina, Saskatchewan

On cool days, which we get plenty of here, I like to get out my slow cooker and make up a batch of this comforting stew. Trying to appeal to 10 picky eaters in our large household is not too easy, but with this recipe, everyone digs right in.

summer's bounty soup

COOK TIME: 7 TO 8 HOURS

- 4 medium tomatoes, chopped
- 2 medium potatoes, peeled and cubed
- 2 cups halved fresh green beans
- 2 small zucchini, cubed
- 1 medium yellow summer squash, cubed
- 4 small carrots, thinly sliced
- 2 celery ribs, thinly sliced
- 1 cup cubed peeled eggplant
- 1 cup sliced fresh mushrooms
- 1 small onion, chopped
- 1 tablespoon minced fresh parsley
- 1 tablespoon salt-free garlic and herb seasoning
- 4 cups V8 juice

Combine all ingredients in a 5-qt. slow cooker. Cover and cook on low for 7-8 hours or until the vegetables are tender.

YIELD: 12-14 SERVINGS (ABOUT 3½ QUARTS).

Victoria Zmarzley-Hahn, Northampton, Pennsylvania

Lots of wonderfully fresh-tasting vegetables are showcased in this chunky soup. It's a great way to use up summer's excess produce. And it's so versatile—you can add or delete any vegetable to suit your taste.

hearty bean soup

Alice Schnoor, Arion, Iowa

This thick soup, with dried beans, ham and vegetables, makes a tasty main dish or a satisfying first course.

COOK TIME: 6 TO 7 HOURS

- 3 cups chopped parsnips
- 2 cups chopped carrots
- 1 cup chopped onion
- 1½ cups dried great northern beans
- 5 cups water
- 1½ pounds smoked ham hocks *or* ham shanks
- 2 garlic cloves, minced
- 2 teaspoons salt
- ½ teaspoon pepper
- ⅛ to ¼ teaspoon hot pepper sauce

1 In a 5-qt. slow cooker, place parsnips, carrots and onion. Top with beans. Add water, ham, garlic, salt, pepper and hot pepper sauce. Cover and cook on high for 6-7 hours or until beans are tender.

2 Remove meat and bones when cool enough to handle. Cut meat into bite-size pieces and return to slow cooker; heat through.

YIELD: 6 SERVINGS.

texican chili

COOK TIME: 9 TO 10 HOURS

8 bacon strips, diced

2½ pounds beef stew meat, cut into ½-inch cubes

2 cans (one 28 ounces, one 14½ ounces) stewed tomatoes

2 cans (8 ounces *each*) tomato sauce

1 can (16 ounces) kidney beans, rinsed and drained

2 cups sliced carrots

1 medium onion, chopped

1 cup chopped celery

½ cup chopped green pepper

¼ cup minced fresh parsley

1 tablespoon chili powder

1 teaspoon salt

½ teaspoon ground cumin

¼ teaspoon pepper

1 In a skillet, cook bacon until crisp. Remove to paper towel to drain. Brown beef in the drippings over medium heat; drain.

2 Transfer to a 5-qt. slow cooker; add bacon and remaining ingredients. Cover and cook on low for 9-10 hours or until the meat is tender, stirring occasionally.

YIELD: 16-18 SERVINGS.

Stacy Law, Cornish, Utah

This flavorful, meaty chili is my favorite...and it's so easy to prepare in the slow cooker. It's a great way to serve a crowd without last-minute preparation. I got the idea from my mother, who used her slow cooker often for soups and stews.

potato chowder

COOK TIME: 8 TO 10 HOURS

  8 cups diced potatoes

$\frac{1}{3}$ cup chopped onion

  3 cans ($14\frac{1}{2}$ ounces *each*) chicken broth

  1 can ($10\frac{3}{4}$ ounces) condensed cream of chicken soup, undiluted

$\frac{1}{4}$ teaspoon pepper

  1 package (8 ounces) cream cheese, cubed

$\frac{1}{2}$ pound sliced bacon, cooked and crumbled, optional

Snipped chives, optional

In a slow cooker, combine the first five ingredients. Cover and cook on low for 8-10 hours or until potatoes are tender. Add cream cheese; stir until blended. Garnish with bacon and chives if desired.

YIELD: 12 SERVINGS (3 QUARTS).

Anna Mayer, Ft. Branch, Indiana

One of the ladies in our church quilting group brought this savory potato soup to a meeting. It's easy to assemble in the morning, then cook all day.

fresh pumpkin soup

Jane Shapton, Portland, Oregon
This appealing soup harvests the comforting fall flavors of just-picked pumpkins and tart apples. A generous bowlful is sure to warm you up on a crisp autumn day.

COOK TIME: 8 TO 10 HOURS

8 cups chopped fresh pumpkin (about 3 pounds)

4 cups chicken broth

3 small tart apples, peeled and chopped

1 medium onion, chopped

2 tablespoons lemon juice

2 tablespoons minced fresh gingerroot

2 garlic cloves, minced

½ teaspoon salt

TOASTED PUMPKIN SEEDS:

½ cup pumpkin seeds

1 teaspoon canola oil

⅛ teaspoon salt

1 In a slow cooker, combine the first eight ingredients; mix well. Cover and cook on low for 8-10 hours or until pumpkin and apples are tender. Meanwhile, toss pumpkin seeds with oil and salt. Spread in an ungreased 15-in. x 10-in. x 1-in. baking pan. Bake at 250° for 50-60 minutes or until golden brown. Set aside.

2 Cool the pumpkin mixture slightly; process in batches in a blender or food processor. Transfer to a large saucepan; heat through. Garnish with toasted pumpkin seeds.

YIELD: 9 SERVINGS.

broth or bouillon?

Broth and bouillon are interchangeable. Broth is quicker, since it's ready to pour. However, one bouillon cube or 1 teaspoon of granules dissolved in 1 cup of boiling water may be substituted for 1 cup of broth in any recipe.

chicken stew over biscuits

COOK TIME: 8 TO 9 HOURS

- 2 envelopes chicken gravy mix
- 2 cups water
- ¾ cup white wine *or* chicken broth
- 2 garlic cloves, minced
- 1 tablespoon minced fresh parsley
- 1 to 2 teaspoons chicken bouillon granules
- ½ teaspoon pepper
- 5 medium carrots, cut into 1-inch chunks
- 1 large onion, cut into eight wedges
- 1 broiler/fryer chicken (3 to 4 pounds), cut up
- 3 tablespoons all-purpose flour
- ⅓ cup cold water
- 1 tube (7½ ounces) refrigerated buttermilk biscuits

1 In a slow cooker, combine gravy mix, water, wine or broth, garlic, parsley, bouillon and pepper until blended. Add the carrots, onion and chicken. Cover and cook on low for 7-8 hours. Increase heat to high.

2 In a small bowl, combine the flour and cold water until smooth; gradually stir into slow cooker. Cover and cook for 1 hour. Meanwhile, bake biscuits according to package directions. Place biscuits in soup bowls; top with stew.

YIELD: 4-6 SERVINGS.

Kathy Garrett, Browns Mills, New Jersey

A pleasant sauce coats this chicken and veggie dinner that's slow cooked to tender perfection, then served over biscuits.

curried lentil soup

COOK TIME: 8 HOURS

- 4 cups hot water
- 1 can (28 ounces) crushed tomatoes
- 3 medium potatoes, peeled and diced
- 3 medium carrots, thinly sliced
- 1 large onion, chopped
- 1 celery rib, chopped
- 1 cup lentils
- 2 garlic cloves, minced
- 2 bay leaves
- 4 teaspoons curry powder
- 1½ teaspoons salt

In a slow cooker, combine all ingredients; stir well. Cover and cook on low for 8 hours or until vegetables and lentils are tender. Discard the bay leaves before serving.

YIELD: 10 SERVINGS (2½ QUARTS).

Christina Till, South Haven, Michigan

Curry gives a different taste sensation to this chili-like soup. It's delicious with a dollop of sour cream. My family welcomes it with open arms—and watering mouths.

beef 'n' black bean soup

COOK TIME: 6 TO 7 HOURS

- 1 pound ground beef
- 2 cans (14½ ounces *each*) chicken broth
- 1 can (14½ ounces) diced tomatoes, undrained
- 8 green onions, thinly sliced
- 3 medium carrots, thinly sliced
- 2 celery ribs, thinly sliced
- 2 garlic cloves, minced
- 1 tablespoon sugar
- 1½ teaspoons dried basil
- ½ teaspoon salt
- ½ teaspoon dried oregano
- ½ teaspoon ground cumin
- ½ teaspoon chili powder
- 2 cans (15 ounces *each*) black beans, rinsed and drained
- 1½ cups cooked rice

1 In a skillet over medium heat, cook beef until no longer pink; drain. Transfer to a slow cooker. Add the next 12 ingredients. Cover and cook on high for 1 hour.

2 Reduce heat to low; cook for 4-5 hours or until vegetables are tender. Add the beans and rice; cook 1 hour longer or until heated through.

YIELD: 10 SERVINGS (2½ QUARTS).

Vickie Gibson, Gardendale, Alabama

I lead a busy life, so I'm always trying to come up with time saving recipes.

This zesty and colorful soup is one of my husband's favorites.

It has been a hit at family gatherings, too.

white chili

COOK TIME: 8 TO 10 HOURS

- 2 medium onions, chopped
- 4 garlic cloves, minced
- 2 quarts water
- 3 pounds chicken breasts *or* thighs, skin removed
- 1 pound dried navy beans
- 2 cans (4 ounces *each*) chopped green chilies
- 1 tablespoon ground cumin
- 2 teaspoons dried oregano
- 1 teaspoon salt
- ½ to 1 teaspoon cayenne pepper
- ½ teaspoon ground cloves
- 2 chicken bouillon cubes

Shredded Monterey Jack cheese

Sour cream

Dried chives and crushed red pepper flakes

1 Place the onions and garlic in a slow cooker. Add the next 10 ingredients; do not stir. Cook on high for 8-10 hours.

2 Uncover and stir (the meat should fall off the bones). Remove bones. Stir to break up the meat. Spoon into bowls; top with cheese and sour cream if desired, and sprinkle with chives and pepper flakes.

YIELD: 12 SERVINGS (3 QUARTS).

Lana Rutledge, Shepherdsville, Kentucky

This savory white chili simmers all day on the kitchen countertop. When your hungry clan calls for dinner, you can ladle up steaming bowlfuls in a hurry. It's a wonderful alternative to traditional tomato-based chilies.

spicy pork chili

Taste of Home Test Kitchen, Greendale, Wisconsin
Slow-cooked boneless pork makes a tasty chili. Adding the corn and black beans brightens up the dish.

COOK TIME: 6 HOURS

2 pounds boneless pork, cut into ½-inch cubes

1 tablespoon vegetable oil

1 can (28 ounces) crushed tomatoes

2 cups frozen corn

1 can (15 ounces) black beans, rinsed and drained

1 cup chopped onion

1 cup beef broth

1 can (4 ounces) chopped green chilies

1 tablespoon chili powder

1 teaspoon minced garlic

½ teaspoon salt

½ teaspoon cayenne pepper

½ teaspoon pepper

¼ cup minced fresh cilantro

Shredded cheddar cheese, optional

1 In a large skillet, cook pork in oil over medium-high heat for 5-6 minutes or until browned. Transfer pork and drippings to a 5-qt. slow cooker.

2 Stir in the tomatoes, corn, beans, onion, broth, chilies, chili powder, garlic, salt, cayenne and pepper. Cover and cook on low for 6 hours or until pork is tender. Stir in cilantro. Serve with cheese if desired.

YIELD: 6 SERVINGS.

potato minestrone

COOK TIME: 8 HOURS

- 2 cans (14-1/2 ounces *each*) chicken broth
- 1 can (28 ounces) crushed tomatoes
- 1 can (16 ounces) kidney beans, rinsed and drained
- 1 can (15 ounces) garbanzo beans *or* chickpeas, rinsed and drained
- 1 can (14-1/2 ounces) beef broth
- 2 cups frozen cubed hash brown potatoes, thawed
- 1 tablespoon dried minced onion
- 1 tablespoon dried parsley flakes
- 1 teaspoon salt
- 1 teaspoon dried oregano
- 1/2 teaspoon garlic powder
- 1/2 teaspoon dried basil
- 1/2 teaspoon dried marjoram
- 1 package (10 ounces) frozen chopped spinach, thawed and drained
- 2 cups frozen peas and carrots, thawed

In a slow cooker, combine the first 13 ingredients. Cover and cook on low for 8 hours. Stir in the spinach, peas and carrots; heat through.

YIELD: 12 SERVINGS (ABOUT 3 QUARTS).

Paula Zsiray, Logan, Utah

With this savory soup, I just add bread and a salad to have dinner ready.

For a thicker soup, mash half of the garbanzo beans and add to the slow cooker.

hearty tomato pasta soup

COOK TIME: 3½ TO 4½ HOURS

1 pound bulk Italian sausage

6 cups beef broth

1 can (28 ounces) stewed tomatoes

1 can (15 ounces) tomato sauce

2 cups sliced zucchini

1 large onion, chopped

1 cup sliced carrots

1 cup sliced fresh mushrooms

1 medium green pepper, chopped

¼ cup minced fresh parsley

2 teaspoons sugar

1 teaspoon dried oregano

1 teaspoon dried basil

1 garlic clove, minced

2 cups frozen cheese tortellini

Grated Parmesan cheese, optional

1 In a skillet, cook the sausage over medium heat until no longer pink; drain. Transfer to a 5-qt. slow cooker; add the next 13 ingredients. Cover and cook on high for 3-4 hours or until the vegetables are tender.

2 Cook tortellini according to package directions; drain. Stir into slow cooker; cover and cook 30 minutes longer. Serve with Parmesan cheese if desired.

YIELD: 14 SERVINGS (ABOUT 3½ QUARTS).

Lydia Kroese, Minnetonka, Minnesota

I adapted the original recipe for this satisfying soup so I could make it in the slow cooker. It's ideal for staff luncheons at the school where I work, since we don't have easy access to a stove or oven.

hamburger vegetable soup

COOK TIME: 8 TO 9 HOURS

- 1 pound ground beef
- 1 medium onion, chopped
- 2 garlic cloves, minced
- 4 cups V8 juice
- 1 can (14½ ounces) stewed tomatoes
- 2 cups coleslaw mix
- 2 cups frozen green beans
- 2 cups frozen corn
- 2 tablespoons Worcestershire sauce
- 1 teaspoon dried basil
- ½ teaspoon salt
- ¼ teaspoon pepper

1 In a saucepan, cook beef, onion and garlic over medium heat until meat is no longer pink; drain.

2 In a slow cooker, combine remaining ingredients. Stir in beef mixture. Cover and cook on low for 8-9 hours or until the vegetables are tender.

YIELD: 10 SERVINGS.

Theresa Jackson, Cicero, New York

I work full time and have a family of four. We sit down to a home-cooked meal just about every night, many times thanks to my slow cooker. This soup is often on the menu.

slow-cooked chunky chili

COOK TIME: 4 TO 5 HOURS

1 **pound ground beef**

1 **pound bulk pork sausage**

4 **cans (16 ounces** *each***) kidney beans, rinsed and drained**

2 **cans (14½ ounces** *each***) diced tomatoes, undrained**

2 **cans (10 ounces** *each***) diced tomatoes and green chilies, undrained**

1 **large onion, chopped**

1 **medium green pepper, chopped**

1 **envelope taco seasoning**

½ **teaspoon salt**

¼ **teaspoon pepper**

In a skillet, cook beef and sausage over medium heat until meat is no longer pink; drain. Transfer to a 5-qt. slow cooker. Stir in the remaining ingredients. Cover and cook on high for 4-5 hours or until the vegetables are tender.

YIELD: 3 QUARTS (12 SERVINGS).

Margie Shaw, Greenbrier, Arkansas

Pork sausage, ground beef and plenty of beans make this chili a hearty meal-starter. I serve bowls of it on cold days—or use it to fix chili dogs, tacos and more.

rich french onion soup

Linda Adolph, Edmonton, Alberta

When entertaining guests, I bring out this tried-and-true soup while we're waiting for the main course. It's simple to make—just saute the onions early in the day and let the soup simmer until dinnertime.

COOK TIME: 5 TO 7 HOURS

6 large onions, chopped

1/2 cup butter

6 cans (10 1/2 ounces *each*) condensed beef broth, undiluted

1 1/2 teaspoons Worcestershire sauce

3 bay leaves

10 slices French bread, toasted

Shredded Parmesan and part-skim mozzarella cheeses

1 In a large skillet, saute onions in butter until crisp-tender. Transfer to an ungreased 5-qt. slow cooker. Add the broth, Worcestershire sauce and bay leaves.

2 Cover and cook on low for 5-7 hours or until the onions are tender. Discard bay leaves. Top each serving with French bread and cheeses.

YIELD: 10 SERVINGS.

faster slow cooking

To speed up cooking time on most slow cooker recipes, including soups and stews, follow the general rule that 1 hour on high is equal to 2 hours on low.

busy day beef stew

COOK TIME: 10 HOURS

- 1 boneless beef chuck roast (1 to 1-1/2 pounds)
- 1 envelope onion soup mix
- 2 teaspoons browning sauce, optional
- 1/2 teaspoon salt
- 1/2 teaspoon pepper
- 6 cups water
- 2 cups cubed peeled potatoes (1/2-inch pieces)
- 6 to 8 medium carrots, cut into chunks
- 1 medium onion, chopped
- 1 cup frozen peas, thawed
- 1 cup frozen corn, thawed
- 5 tablespoons cornstarch
- 6 tablespoons cold water

1 Place roast in a slow cooker; sprinkle with soup mix, browning sauce if desired, salt and pepper. Pour water over meat. Cover and cook on low for 8 hours.

2 Remove roast to a cutting board; let stand for 5 minutes. Add vegetables to slow cooker. Cube beef and return to slow cooker. Cover and cook on low for 1-1/2 hours or until vegetables are tender. Combine cornstarch and cold water until smooth; stir into stew. Cover and cook on high for 30-45 minutes or until thickened.

YIELD: 8-10 SERVINGS.

Beth Wyatt, Paris, Kentucky

I call this my "lazy" stew because it's so easy to make on busy days. It keeps folks coming back for more.

hominy pork soup

COOK TIME: 4 HOURS

1 pound pork chop suey meat, cut into 1/2-inch cubes

2 cans (15 ounces *each*) chili without beans

1 can (15 1/2 ounces) hominy, drained

1 can (8 ounces) tomato sauce

1 medium onion, chopped

1 bay leaf

1 tablespoon chili powder

1 teaspoon *each* dried basil, oregano and parsley flakes

1 teaspoon ground cumin

Warmed flour tortillas, shredded Monterey Jack cheese, sliced green onions and lime wedges, optional

1 In a slow cooker, combine the pork, chili, hominy, tomato sauce, onion and seasonings. Cover and cook on high for 4 hours or until meat is tender.

2 Discard bay leaf. Serve with tortillas, cheese, green onions and lime wedges if desired.

YIELD: 7 SERVINGS.

Raquel Walkup, San Pedro, California

Tender pork and hominy make this chili-like soup different from the usual offerings. It's an easy-to-prepare yet satisfying supper.

green chili stew

Jacqueline Thompson Graves, Lawrenceville, Georgia

This stew is much heartier than most—and very tasty, too. My family especially enjoys the zippy broth and the generous amounts of tender beef. They frequently request second helpings.

COOK TIME: 7 TO 8 HOURS

- 2 pounds beef stew meat, cut into 1-inch cubes
- 2 medium onions, chopped
- 2 tablespoons vegetable oil
- 1 can (15 ounces) pinto beans, rinsed and drained
- 1 can (14½ ounces) diced tomatoes, undrained
- 2 cans (4 ounces *each*) chopped green chilies
- 1 cup water
- 3 beef bouillon cubes
- 1 garlic clove, minced
- 1 teaspoon sugar
- ½ teaspoon salt
- ¼ teaspoon pepper

Shredded cheddar *or* Monterey Jack cheese, optional

1 In a skillet, brown beef and onions in oil; drain. Transfer to a 5-qt. slow cooker.

2 Combine beans, tomatoes, chilies, water, bouillon, garlic, sugar, salt and pepper; pour over beef. Cover; cook on low for 7-8 hours or until beef is tender. Sprinkle with cheese if desired.

YIELD: 8 SERVINGS.

texas black bean soup

COOK TIME: 4 TO 5 HOURS

  2 cans (15 ounces *each*) black beans, rinsed and drained

  1 can (14½ ounces) stewed tomatoes *or* Mexican stewed tomatoes, cut up

  1 can (14½ ounces) diced tomatoes *or* diced tomatoes with green chilies

  1 can (14½ ounces) chicken broth

  1 can (11 ounces) Mexicorn, drained

  2 cans (4 ounces *each*) chopped green chilies

  4 green onions, thinly sliced

  2 to 3 tablespoons chili powder

  1 teaspoon ground cumin

½ teaspoon dried minced garlic

In a slow cooker, combine all ingredients. Cover and cook on high for 4-5 hours or until heated through.

YIELD: 8-10 SERVINGS (ABOUT 2½ QUARTS).

Pamela Scott, Garland, Texas

This hearty soup made with convenient canned items is perfect for spicing up a family gathering on a cool day. It tastes great and requires so little time and attention.

hearty pork stew

COOK TIME: 8½ HOURS

1½ to 2 pounds boneless pork, cut into 1-inch cubes

4 cups water

1 can (14½ ounces) stewed tomatoes

1 medium onion, chopped

1 medium green pepper, chopped

⅓ cup soy sauce

1 to 2 tablespoons chili powder

1 tablespoon dried celery flakes

½ teaspoon garlic powder

½ teaspoon pepper

⅓ cup cornstarch

⅓ cup cold water

Hot cooked noodles

1 In a slow cooker, combine the first 10 ingredients. Cover and cook on low for 8 hours.

2 Combine cornstarch and water until smooth; gradually stir into slow cooker. Cover and cook on high for 30 minutes or until slightly thickened. Serve in bowls over noodles.

YIELD: 8-10 SERVINGS.

Rebecca Overy, Evanston, Wyoming

Tender chunks of pork combine with colorful tomatoes and green peppers in this savory stew. I garnish bowls of it with chopped, hard-cooked eggs and green onions.

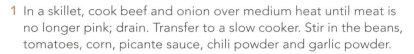

corny chili

COOK TIME: 3 TO 4 HOURS

1 pound ground beef

1 small onion, chopped

1 can (16 ounces) kidney beans, rinsed and drained

2 cans (14½ ounces *each*) diced tomatoes, undrained

1 can (11 ounces) whole kernel corn, drained

¾ cup picante sauce

1 tablespoon chili powder

¼ to ½ teaspoon garlic powder

Corn chips, sour cream and shredded cheddar cheese, optional

1 In a skillet, cook beef and onion over medium heat until meat is no longer pink; drain. Transfer to a slow cooker. Stir in the beans, tomatoes, corn, picante sauce, chili powder and garlic powder.

2 Cover and cook on low for 3-4 hours or until heated through. Serve with corn chips, sour cream and cheese if desired.

YIELD: 4-6 SERVINGS.

Marlene Olson, Hoople, North Dakota

This is so delicious and simple that I had to share it. I'm sure busy moms will be just as happy as I am with the taste and time-saving convenience of this pleasant chili.

trout chowder

COOK TIME: 1½ TO 2 HOURS

- 1 medium onion, chopped
- 1 tablespoon butter
- 2 cups milk
- 1 cup ranch salad dressing
- 1 pound boneless trout fillets, skin removed
- 1 package (10 ounces) frozen broccoli cuts, thawed
- 1 cup cubed *or* shredded cheddar cheese
- 1 cup cubed *or* shredded Monterey Jack cheese
- ¼ teaspoon garlic powder

Paprika, optional

1 In a skillet, saute onion in butter until tender. Transfer to a slow cooker; add milk, dressing, fish, broccoli, cheeses and garlic powder.

2 Cover and cook on high for 1½ to 2 hours or until soup is bubbly and fish flakes easily with a fork. Sprinkle with paprika if desired.

YIELD: 6 SERVINGS.

Linda Kesselring, Corning, New York
This hearty chowder cooks in a slow cooker, so I can spend more time fishing and less in the kitchen. Broccoli adds fresh taste and lively color to the rich, cheesy broth.

chicken mushroom stew

Kim Marie Van Rheenen, Mendota, Illinois

As it simmers, the flavors blend beautifully in this pot of chicken, vegetables and herbs. This stew always draws compliments from those who try it.

COOK TIME: 4 HOURS

- 6 **boneless skinless chicken breast halves (1½ pounds)**
- 2 **tablespoons vegetable oil, *divided***
- 8 **ounces fresh mushrooms, sliced**
- 1 **medium onion, diced**
- 3 **cups diced zucchini**
- 1 **cup diced green pepper**
- 4 **garlic cloves, minced**
- 3 **medium tomatoes, diced**
- 1 **can (6 ounces) tomato paste**
- ¾ **cup water**
- 2 **teaspoons salt**
- 1 **teaspoon *each* dried thyme, oregano, marjoram and basil**

1 Cut chicken into 1-in. cubes; brown in 1 tablespoon oil in a large skillet. Transfer to a slow cooker. In the same skillet, saute the mushrooms, onion, zucchini, green pepper and garlic in remaining oil until crisp-tender. Place in slow cooker.

2 Add tomatoes, tomato paste, water and seasonings. Cover and cook on low for 4 hours or until the vegetables are tender.

YIELD: 6 SERVINGS.

meaty tomato soup

COOK TIME: 8 HOURS

- 1 can (28 ounces) diced tomatoes, undrained
- 2 cans (8 ounces *each*) tomato sauce
- 2 cups water
- ½ pound ground beef, cooked and drained
- ½ pound bulk pork sausage, cooked and drained
- 2 tablespoons dried minced onion
- 2 chicken bouillon cubes
- ¾ teaspoon garlic salt
- ¾ cup uncooked elbow macaroni

Shredded cheddar cheese, optional

1 In a slow cooker, combine the first eight ingredients; mix well. Cover and cook on low for 8 hours. Add macaroni and mix well.

2 Cover and cook 15 minutes longer or until macaroni is tender. Garnish with cheese if desired.

YIELD: 8-10 SERVINGS (2¼ QUARTS).

Ann Bost, Elkhart, Texas

As an elementary school librarian and church choir director, I've come to rely on and thoroughly enjoy slow-cooked meals. A sorority sister shared this recipe with me.

minestrone stew

COOK TIME: 4 TO 6 HOURS

- 1 **pound ground beef**
- 1 **small onion, chopped**
- 1 **can (19 ounces) ready-to-serve minestrone soup**
- 1 **can (15 ounces) pinto beans, rinsed and drained**
- 1 **can (14½ ounces) stewed tomatoes**
- 1 **can (11 ounces) whole kernel corn, drained**
- 1 **can (4 ounces) chopped green chilies**
- 1 **teaspoon salt**
- ½ **teaspoon garlic powder**
- ½ **teaspoon onion powder**

In a skillet, cook beef and onion over medium heat until meat is no longer pink; drain. Transfer to a slow cooker. Add the remaining ingredients; mix well. Cover and cook on low for 4-6 hours or until heated through.

YIELD: 8 SERVINGS.

Janie Hoskins, Red Bluff, California

This stew is made from convenient pantry ingredients, plus it's easy on the pocketbook. You're sure to like the taste.

slow cooker vegetable soup

COOK TIME: 8 HOURS

1 pound boneless round steak, cut into ½-inch cubes

1 can (14½ ounces) diced tomatoes, undrained

3 cups water

2 medium potatoes, peeled and cubed

2 medium onions, diced

3 celery ribs, sliced

2 carrots, sliced

3 beef bouillon cubes

½ teaspoon dried basil

½ teaspoon dried oregano

½ teaspoon salt

¼ teaspoon pepper

1½ cups frozen mixed vegetables

1 In a slow cooker, combine the first 12 ingredients. Cover and cook on high for 6 hours.

2 Add vegetables; cover and cook on high 2 hours longer or until the meat and vegetables are tender.

YIELD: 8-10 SERVINGS (ABOUT 2½ QUARTS).

Heather Thurmeier, Pense, Saskatchewan

What a treat it is to come home from work and have this satisfying soup simmering away. It's a nice, traditional beef soup with old-fashioned goodness. We pair it with fresh crusty rolls topped with melted mozzarella cheese.

manhattan clam chowder

COOK TIME: 8 TO 10 HOURS

3 celery ribs, sliced

1 large onion, chopped

1 can (14½ ounces) sliced potatoes, drained

1 can (14½ ounces) sliced carrots, drained

2 cans (6½ ounces *each*) chopped clams

2 cups tomato juice

1½ cups water

½ cup tomato puree

1 tablespoon dried parsley flakes

1½ teaspoons dried thyme

1 teaspoon salt

1 bay leaf

2 whole black peppercorns

In a slow cooker, combine all ingredients; stir. Cover and cook on low for 8-10 hours or until the vegetables are tender. Remove bay leaf and peppercorns before serving.

YIELD: 9 SERVINGS.

Mary Dixon, Northville, Michigan

I came up with this delicious soup years ago when my husband and I both worked. It's easy to dump all the ingredients into the slow cooker in the morning…and great to come home to the aroma of dinner ready.

chili in bread bowls

Nancy Clancy, Standish, Maine

Some say you can have your cake and eat it, too…I say eat your chili and the bowl, too! I work the "graveyard shift" at the post office in Portland. During those hours, there is no place to buy meals, so I often bring in dishes like this.

COOK TIME: 7 TO 8 HOURS

- 1 tablespoon all-purpose flour
- ¼ teaspoon salt
- ⅛ teaspoon pepper
- ½ pound *each* lean beef stew meat, boneless skinless chicken breast and boneless pork, cut into cubes
- 1 tablespoon vegetable oil
- 1 medium onion, chopped
- 1 medium green pepper, chopped
- 1 jalapeno pepper, seeded and chopped
- 1 can (28 ounces) diced tomatoes, drained
- 1 can (16 ounces) kidney beans, rinsed and drained
- 1 can (15½ ounces) navy beans *or* great northern beans, rinsed and drained
- 1 can (8 ounces) tomato sauce
- 1 tablespoon chili powder
- 1 garlic clove, minced
- 1½ teaspoons ground cumin
- ½ teaspoon dried basil
- ¼ to ½ teaspoon cayenne pepper
- 9 large hard rolls

Sour cream, chopped green onions and sweet red pepper, optional

1 In a large resealable plastic bag, combine the flour, salt and pepper. Add meat in batches; toss to coat. In a large skillet, brown meat in oil in batches.

2 Transfer to a 5-qt. slow cooker with a slotted spoon. Stir in onion, peppers, tomatoes, beans, tomato sauce and seasonings. Cover and cook on low for 7-8 hours or until meat is tender.

3 Cut tops off rolls; carefully hollow out bottom halves. Spoon about 1 cup of chili into each roll. Garnish with sour cream, onions and red pepper if desired.

YIELD: 9 SERVINGS.

EDITOR'S NOTE: When cutting or seeding hot peppers, use rubber or plastic gloves to protect your hands. Avoid touching your face.

buffalo chicken wing soup

COOK TIME: 4 TO 5 HOURS

- 6 cups milk
- 3 cans (10¾ ounces *each*) condensed cream of chicken soup, undiluted
- 3 cups shredded cooked chicken (about 1 pound)
- 1 cup (8 ounces) sour cream
- ¼ to ½ cup hot pepper sauce

Combine all ingredients in a slow cooker. Cover and cook on low for 4-5 hours.

YIELD: 8 SERVINGS (2 QUARTS).

Pat Farmer, Falconer, New York

Start with a small amount of hot sauce, then add more if needed to suit your family's tastes.

spicy beef vegetable soup

COOK TIME: 8 HOURS

- 1 pound ground beef
- 1 cup chopped onion
- 1 jar (30 ounces) meatless spaghetti sauce
- 3½ cups water
- 1 package (16 ounces) frozen mixed vegetables
- 1 can (10 ounces) diced tomatoes and green chilies
- 1 cup sliced celery
- 1 teaspoon beef bouillon granules
- 1 teaspoon pepper

1 In a skillet over medium heat, cook beef and onion until meat is no longer pink; drain. Transfer to a slow cooker. Stir in the remaining ingredients.

2 Cover and cook on low for 8 hours or until the vegetables are tender.

YIELD: 12 SERVINGS (3 QUARTS).

Lynnette Davis, Tullahoma, Tennessee

This savory ground beef and vegetable soup is flavorful and fast to fix.

It makes a complete meal when served with warm corn bread, sourdough bread or French bread.

savory sandwiches

87

96

Scoop, stuff, fold, wrap or layer…however you want to build your sandwich, start with these tempting two-handed creations! For get-togethers on game day, make a tangy batch of Beef Barbecue (p. 87). Or surprise your family with sweet and spicy Hearty Italian Sandwiches (p. 96).

Turn to any of these super sandwich solutions when you want to spend less time in the kitchen and more time with your family. If you're lucky, you might even have leftovers to enjoy the next day!

herbed french dip sandwiches

COOK TIME: 10 TO 12 HOURS

1 lean beef roast (3 to 4 pounds)

½ cup soy sauce

1 beef bouillon cube

1 bay leaf

3 to 4 whole peppercorns

1 teaspoon dried rosemary, crushed

1 teaspoon dried thyme

1 teaspoon garlic powder

Hard rolls *or* French bread

1 Remove and discard all visible fat from roast. Place in a slow cooker. Combine soy sauce, bouillon and spices; pour over roast. Add water to almost cover roast. Cover and cook over low heat for 10-12 hours or until meat is very tender.

2 Remove meat and discard bay leaf; reserve cooking juices. Shred meat with two forks. Serve on hard rolls or French bread slices. Serve cooking juices as a dipping sauce.

YIELD: 12 SERVINGS.

Dianne Joy Richardson, Colorado Springs, Colorado

I found this recipe in one of our local publications. It's great for an easy meal any time of year, since the meat cooks all day without any attention.

beef barbecue

COOK TIME: 6½ TO 8½ HOURS

- 1 boneless chuck roast (3 pounds)
- 1 cup barbecue sauce
- ½ cup apricot preserves
- ⅓ cup chopped green *or* sweet red pepper
- 1 small onion, chopped
- 1 tablespoon Dijon mustard
- 2 teaspoons brown sugar
- 12 sandwich rolls, split

1 Cut the roast into quarters; place in a greased 5-qt. slow cooker. In a bowl, combine barbecue sauce, preserves, green pepper, onion, mustard and brown sugar; pour over roast. Cover and cook on low for 6-8 hours or until meat is tender.

2 Remove roast and thinly slice; return meat to slow cooker and stir gently. Cover and cook 20-30 minutes longer. Skim fat from sauce. Serve beef and sauce on rolls.

YIELD: 12 SERVINGS.

Karen Walker, Sterling, Virginia

When we're not in the mood for pot roast, I prepare these satisfying sandwiches instead. The meat cooks in a tasty sauce while I'm away at work. Then I just slice it thinly and serve it on rolls.

sausage pepper sandwiches

Suzette Gessel, Albuquerque, New Mexico

Peppers and onions add a fresh taste to this zippy sausage filling for sandwiches. My mother gave me this recipe. It's simple to assemble, and it's gobbled up quickly.

COOK TIME: 8 HOURS

 5 uncooked Italian sausage links (about 20 ounces)

 1 medium green pepper, cut into 1-inch pieces

 1 large onion, cut into 1-inch pieces

 1 can (8 ounces) tomato sauce

 1/8 teaspoon pepper

 6 hoagie *or* submarine sandwich buns, split

1 In a large skillet, brown sausage links over medium heat. Cut into 1/2-in. slices; place in a 3-qt. slow cooker. Stir in the green pepper, onion, tomato sauce and pepper.

2 Cover and cook on low for 8 hours or until sausage is no longer pink and vegetables are tender. Use a slotted spoon to serve on buns.

YIELD: 6 SERVINGS.

tangy barbecue sandwiches

COOK TIME: 7 TO 8 HOURS

- 3 cups chopped celery
- 1 cup chopped onion
- 1 cup ketchup
- 1 cup barbecue sauce
- 1 cup water
- 2 tablespoons vinegar
- 2 tablespoons Worcestershire sauce
- 2 tablespoons brown sugar
- 1 teaspoon chili powder
- 1 teaspoon salt
- 1/2 teaspoon pepper
- 1/2 teaspoon garlic powder
- 1 boneless chuck roast (3 to 4 pounds), trimmed
- 14 to 18 hamburger buns, split

In a slow cooker, combine the first 12 ingredients; mix well. Add roast. Cover and cook on high for 7-8 hours or until meat is tender. Remove roast; cool. Shred meat and return to sauce; heat through. Use a slotted spoon to serve on buns.

YIELD: 14-18 SERVINGS.

Debbi Smith, Crossett, Arkansas

Since I prepare the beef for these robust sandwiches in a slow cooker, it's easy to fix a meal for a hungry bunch. The savory homemade sauce ensures I come home with no leftovers from potluck dinners and other gatherings.

teriyaki sandwiches

COOK TIME: 7 TO 9 HOURS

2 pounds boneless chuck steak

1/4 cup soy sauce

1 tablespoon brown sugar

1 teaspoon ground ginger

1 garlic clove, minced

4 teaspoons cornstarch

2 tablespoons water

8 French rolls, split

1/4 cup butter, melted

Pineapple rings

Chopped green onions

1 Cut steak into thin slices. In a slow cooker, combine soy sauce, sugar, ginger and garlic. Add steak. Cover and cook on low for 7-9 hours or until meat is tender. Remove the meat with a slotted spoon; set aside.

2 Carefully pour liquid into a 2-cup measuring cup; skim fat. Add water to liquid to measure 1 1/2 cups. Pour into a large saucepan. Combine cornstarch and water until smooth; add to pan. Cook and stir until thick and bubbly, about 2 minutes. Add meat and heat through.

3 Brush rolls with butter; broil 4-5 in. from the heat for 2-3 minutes or until lightly toasted. Fill with meat, pineapple and green onions.

YIELD: 8 SERVINGS.

Bernice Muilenburg, Molalla, Oregon

The meat for these sandwiches comes out of the slow cooker tender and flavorful. Living as we do in the foothills of the Cascades, we frequently have venison and elk in the freezer. I sometimes substitute that in this recipe, and it never tastes like game.

fiesta pork sandwiches

Yvette Massey, La Luz, New Mexico

This is an easy and flavorful dish that my family really enjoys. When I make these sandwiches for company, I usually prepare the meat the day before, so I can concentrate on side dishes and relaxing with my friends.

COOK TIME: 8 TO 10 HOURS

- 1 boneless pork shoulder roast (3 to 4 pounds)
- 1/3 cup lime juice
- 2 tablespoons grapefruit juice
- 2 tablespoons water
- 1 bay leaf
- 6 garlic cloves, minced
- 1/2 teaspoon salt
- 1/2 teaspoon dried oregano
- 1/2 teaspoon chili powder
- 2 tablespoons olive oil
- 1 large onion, thinly sliced
- 12 to 14 sandwich rolls, split

1 Cut the roast in half; pierce several times with a fork. Place in a large resealable plastic bag or shallow glass container. Combine the next eight ingredients; pour over roast. Cover and refrigerate overnight, turning occasionally.

2 Drain, reserving marinade. In a skillet over medium heat, brown the roast in oil on all sides. Place onion, roast and marinade in a slow cooker. Cover and cook on high for 2 hours.

3 Reduce heat to low; cook 6-8 hours longer or until the meat is tender. Remove roast; shred or thinly slice. Discard the bay leaf. Skim fat from cooking juices and transfer to a saucepan; bring to a rolling boil. Serve pork on rolls with juices as a dipping sauce.

YIELD: 12-14 SERVINGS.

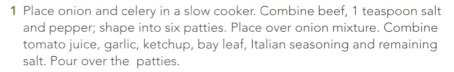

meat loaf burgers

COOK TIME: 7 TO 9 HOURS

- 1 large onion, sliced
- 1 celery rib, chopped
- 2 pounds lean ground beef
- 1½ teaspoons salt, *divided*
- ¼ teaspoon pepper
- 2 cups tomato juice
- 4 garlic cloves, minced
- 1 tablespoon ketchup
- 1 bay leaf
- 1 teaspoon Italian seasoning
- 6 hamburger buns, split

1 Place onion and celery in a slow cooker. Combine beef, 1 teaspoon salt and pepper; shape into six patties. Place over onion mixture. Combine tomato juice, garlic, ketchup, bay leaf, Italian seasoning and remaining salt. Pour over the patties.

2 Cover and cook on low for 7-9 hours or until meat is tender. Discard bay leaf. Separate patties with a spatula if necessary; serve on buns.

YIELD: 6 SERVINGS.

Peggy Burdick, Burlington, Michigan

These hearty sandwiches are great for potluck dinners. The beefy patties get extra flavor from seasoned sauce. They're a fun change from plain burgers and regular meat loaf.

dilly beef sandwiches

COOK TIME: 8 TO 9 HOURS

1 boneless beef chuck roast
  (3 to 4 pounds)

1 jar (16 ounces) whole dill pickles,
  undrained

½ cup chili sauce

2 garlic cloves, minced

10 to 12 hamburger buns, split

1 Cut roast in half and place in a slow cooker. Add pickles with juice, chili sauce and garlic. Cover and cook on low for 8-9 hours or until beef is tender.

2 Discard pickles. Remove roast. When cool enough to handle, shred the meat. Return to the sauce and heat through. Using a slotted spoon, fill each bun with about ½ cup meat mixture.

YIELD: 10-12 SERVINGS.

Donna Blankenheim, Madison, Wisconsin

My sister shared this recipe, which puts a twist on the traditional barbecue sandwich. As a mother of four, she never has much time to cook, but she does like to entertain. This crowd-pleaser, which takes mere minutes to prep, is perfect for our large family gatherings.

hearty italian sandwiches

Elaine Krupsky, Las Vegas, Nevada

I've been making this sweet and spicy sandwich filling for 35 years. It smells as good as it tastes! It's a great reward for a hungry family after a day working or playing outdoors. It's not uncommon to get requests for second helpings.

COOK TIME: 6 HOURS

- 1½ pounds lean ground beef
- 1½ pounds bulk Italian sausage
- 2 large onions, sliced
- 2 large green peppers, sliced
- 2 large sweet red peppers, sliced
- 1 teaspoon salt
- 1 teaspoon pepper
- ¼ teaspoon crushed red pepper flakes
- 8 sandwich rolls, split

Shredded Monterey Jack cheese, optional

1 In a skillet, cook beef and sausage over medium heat until meat is no longer pink; drain. Place a third of the onions and peppers in a slow cooker; top with half of the meat mixture. Repeat layers of vegetables and meat, then top with remaining vegetables. Sprinkle with salt, pepper and pepper flakes.

2 Cover and cook on low for 6 hours or until vegetables are tender. With a slotted spoon, serve about 1 cup of meat and vegetables on each roll. Top with cheese if desired. Use pan juices for dipping if desired.

YIELD: 8 SERVINGS.

italian beef hoagies

COOK TIME: 8 HOURS

- 1 boneless sirloin tip roast (about 4 pounds), halved
- 2 envelopes Italian salad dressing mix
- 2 cups water
- 1 jar (16 ounces) mild pepper rings, undrained
- 18 hoagie buns, split

1 Place roast in a 5-qt. slow cooker. Combine the salad dressing mix and water; pour over roast. Cover and cook on low for 8 hours or until meat is tender.

2 Remove meat; shred with a fork and return to slow cooker. Add pepper rings; heat through. Spoon 1/2 cup meat mixture onto each bun.

YIELD: 18 SERVINGS.

Lori Piatt, Danville, Illinois

You'll need just five ingredients to feed a crowd these tender tangy sandwiches. On weekends, I start the roast the night before, so I can shred it in the morning.

turkey sloppy joes

COOK TIME: 4 HOURS

- 1 pound ground turkey breast
- 1 small onion, chopped
- ½ cup chopped celery
- ¼ cup chopped green pepper
- 1 can (10¾ ounces) condensed tomato soup, undiluted
- ½ cup ketchup
- 1 tablespoon brown sugar
- 2 tablespoons prepared mustard
- ¼ teaspoon pepper
- 8 hamburger buns, split

1 In a large saucepan coated with nonstick cooking spray, cook the turkey, onion, celery and green pepper over medium heat until the meat is no longer pink; drain if necessary. Stir in the soup, ketchup, brown sugar, mustard and pepper.

2 Transfer to a slow cooker. Cover and cook on low for 4 hours. Serve on buns.

YIELD: 8 SERVINGS.

Marylou LaRue, Freeland, Michigan

This tangy sandwich filling is so easy to prepare in the slow cooker, and it goes over well at gatherings large and small. I frequently take it to potlucks, and I'm always asked for my secret ingredient.

teriyaki pulled pork sandwiches

Taste of Home Test Kitchen, Greendale, Wisconsin

The aroma of pork roast slowly cooking in pineapple juice and teriyaki sauce is a nice way to come home at the end of a busy day!

COOK TIME: 7½ TO 8½ HOURS

- 1 boneless pork shoulder roast (3 pounds), trimmed
- 2 teaspoons olive oil
- 1 cup finely chopped onion
- 1 cup teriyaki sauce, *divided*
- ½ cup unsweetened pineapple juice
- 3 tablespoons all-purpose flour
- 8 whole wheat hamburger buns, split
- 1 can (20 ounces) sliced pineapple, drained

1 In a large skillet, brown roast in oil over medium-high heat. Cut in half; place in a 5-qt. slow cooker. Add the onion, ½ cup teriyaki sauce and pineapple juice. Cover and cook on low for 7-8 hours or until meat is tender.

2 Remove roast; set aside. In a small bowl, combine the flour and remaining teriyaki sauce until smooth; stir into cooking juices. Cover and cook on high for 30-40 minutes or until thickened.

3 Shred meat with two forks; return to the slow cooker and heat through. Spoon ½ cup onto each bun; top with a slice of pineapple.

YIELD: 8 SERVINGS.

how to shred meat

For the best results when shredding meat, follow this method:

Remove the cooked meat from the slow cooker, with a slotted spoon if necessary. Reserve the cooking liquid if called for. Place the meat in a shallow pan or platter. With two forks, pull the meat into thin shreds. Return the shredded meat to the slow cooker to warm or use as the recipe directs.

savory beef sandwiches

COOK TIME: 6 TO 8 HOURS

- 1 tablespoon dried minced onion
- 2 teaspoons salt
- 2 teaspoons garlic powder
- 2 teaspoons dried oregano
- 1 teaspoon dried rosemary, crushed
- 1 teaspoon caraway seeds
- 1 teaspoon dried marjoram
- 1 teaspoon celery seed
- 1/4 teaspoon cayenne pepper
- 1 boneless chuck roast (3 to 4 pounds), halved
- 8 to 10 sandwich rolls, split

Combine seasonings; rub over roast. Place in a slow cooker. Cover and cook on low for 6-8 hours or until meat is tender. Shred with a fork. Serve on rolls.

YIELD: 8-10 SERVINGS.

EDITOR'S NOTE: No liquid is added to the slow cooker. The moisture comes from the roast.

Lynn Williamson, Hayward, Wisconsin

Before heading to work in the morning, I'll get this going in the slow cooker. Then it's all ready to serve as soon as my husband and I walk in.

ham barbecue

COOK TIME: 4 TO 5 HOURS

- 2 pounds thinly sliced deli ham
- 1 cup water
- 1 cup ketchup
- ¼ cup packed brown sugar
- ¼ cup Worcestershire sauce
- 2 tablespoons white vinegar
- 2 teaspoons prepared mustard
- 12 hamburger buns, split and toasted

Place the ham in a greased 3-qt. slow cooker. In a bowl, combine the water, ketchup, brown sugar, Worcestershire sauce, vinegar and mustard; pour over ham and stir well. Cover and cook on low for 4-5 hours or until heated through. Serve on buns.

YIELD: 12 SERVINGS.

Jennifer Middlekauff, New Holland, Pennsylvania

We have used this recipe countless times for family gatherings and birthday parties. The sandwiches are so easy to make, and they taste great.

barbecued chicken sandwiches

Roberta Brown, Waupaca, Wisconsin

These sandwiches are great for large gatherings since they have a popular flavor and are convenient to serve. The chicken can be cooked ahead of time, then added to the homemade barbecue sauce for simmering hours before guests arrive.

COOK TIME: 6 TO 8 HOURS

- 2 broiler-fryer chickens (3 to 3½ pounds *each*), cooked and shredded
- 1 large onion, chopped
- 2 cups water
- 1¼ cups ketchup
- ¼ cup packed brown sugar
- ¼ cup Worcestershire sauce
- ¼ cup red wine vinegar
- 1 teaspoon *each* salt, celery seed and chili powder
- ¼ teaspoon hot pepper sauce

Hamburger buns

In a 3-qt. slow cooker, combine the first seven ingredients; add seasonings and hot pepper sauce and mix well. Cook on low for 6-8 hours. Serve on buns.

YIELD: 8-10 SERVINGS.

EDITOR'S NOTE: 6 cups diced cooked chicken may be used instead of the shredded chicken.

savory chicken sandwiches

COOK TIME: 8 TO 9 HOURS

- 4 bone-in chicken breast halves
- 4 chicken thighs
- 1 envelope onion soup mix
- ¼ teaspoon garlic salt
- ¼ cup prepared Italian salad dressing
- ¼ cup water
- 14 to 16 hamburger buns, split

1 Remove skin from chicken if desired. Place chicken in a 5-qt. slow cooker. Sprinkle with soup mix and garlic salt. Pour dressing and water over chicken. Cover and cook on low for 8-9 hours.

2 Remove the chicken; cool slightly. Skim fat from cooking juices. Remove the chicken from bones; cut into bite-size pieces and return to slow cooker. Serve with a slotted spoon on buns.

YIELD: 14-16 SERVINGS.

Joan Parker, Gastonia, North Carolina

This tender chicken tastes like you fussed, but requires few ingredients.

You can also thicken the juices and serve it over rice.

thawing required

Frozen meat should be completely thawed before placing in a slow cooker. Whole roasts and poultry should be cut in half or into smaller pieces to ensure thorough cooking.

brisket for a bunch

COOK TIME: 7 TO 8 HOURS

- 1 beef brisket (2½ pounds), cut in half
- 1 tablespoon vegetable oil
- ½ cup chopped celery
- ½ cup chopped onion
- ¾ cup beef broth
- ½ cup tomato sauce
- ¼ cup water
- ¼ cup sugar
- 2 tablespoons onion soup mix
- 1 tablespoon cider vinegar
- 12 hamburger buns, split

1 In a large skillet, brown the brisket on all sides in oil; transfer to a slow cooker. In the same skillet, saute celery and onion for 1 minute. Gradually add broth, tomato sauce and water; stir to loosen the browned bits from pan. Add sugar, soup mix and vinegar; bring to a boil.

2 Pour over brisket. Cover and cook on low for 7-8 hours or until meat is tender. Let stand for 5 minutes before slicing. Skim fat from cooking juices. Serve meat in buns with cooking juices.

YIELD: 12 SERVINGS.

EDITOR'S NOTE: This recipe is for fresh beef brisket, not corned beef.

Dawn Fagerstrom, Warren, Minnesota

I know your family will enjoy the tender slices of beef and delicious au jus in this recipe. It's a handy way to satisfy a large group.

italian venison sandwiches

COOK TIME: 8 HOURS

2 cups water

1 envelope onion soup mix

1 tablespoon dried basil

1 tablespoon dried parsley flakes

1 teaspoon beef bouillon granules

1/2 teaspoon celery salt

1/4 teaspoon garlic powder

1/4 teaspoon cayenne pepper

1/4 teaspoon pepper

1 boneless venison roast (3 to 4 pounds), cut into 1-inch cubes

10 to 12 sandwich rolls, split

Green pepper rings, optional

In a slow cooker, combine the first nine ingredients. Add venison and stir. Cover and cook on low for 8 hours or until meat is tender. Using a slotted spoon, spoon into rolls. Top with pepper rings if desired.

YIELD: 10-12 SERVINGS.

Andrew Henson, Morrison, Illinois

The slow cooker makes easy work of these hearty venison sandwiches. The meat always comes out tender and tasty. That makes it a favorite for an avid hunter and cook like me.

beef & ground beef

125

129

Beef up your next dinner menu with exceptional entrees from your slow cooker! Longer cook times in the handy appliance produce fall-off-the-bone meats like Throw-Together Short Ribs (p. 125). And even traditional dishes such as Meaty Spaghetti Sauce (p. 129) taste just like originals—only require less stovetop time from you!

Whether you crave a comforting casserole, prefer a succulent roast or are searching for the perfect one-pot meal the whole family will love, turn the work over to the slow cooker when you choose from this delicious batch of recipes.

pepper beef goulash

Peggy Key, Grant, Alabama

I use only a couple of common ingredients to turn beef stew meat into a hearty entree. No one will ever guess the secret behind this great goulash—an envelope of sloppy joe seasoning.

COOK TIME: 4 TO 5 HOURS

½ cup water

1 can (6 ounces) tomato paste

2 tablespoons cider vinegar

1 envelope sloppy joe seasoning

2 to 2¼ pounds beef stew meat (¾-inch cubes)

1 celery rib, cut into ½-inch slices

1 medium green pepper, cut into ½-inch chunks

Hot cooked rice *or* noodles

In a slow cooker, combine the water, tomato paste, vinegar and sloppy joe seasoning. Stir in the beef, celery and green pepper. Cover and cook on high for 4-5 hours. Serve over rice or noodles.

YIELD: 4-5 SERVINGS.

why pay more?

Economical, less tender cuts of beef like round steak, stew meat and cube steak are perfect for the slow cooker. The long, slow cooking process achieved with the use of this handy appliance ensures fork-tender, moist and flavorful meat even on cuts that would be tough and chewy prepared using other cooking methods.

stuffed flank steak

COOK TIME: 6 TO 8 HOURS

1 package (8 ounces) crushed corn bread stuffing

1 cup chopped onion

1 cup chopped celery

1/4 cup minced fresh parsley

2 eggs

1 1/4 cups beef broth

1/3 cup butter, melted

1/2 teaspoon seasoned salt

1/2 teaspoon pepper

1 1/2 pounds flank steak

1 In a large bowl, combine stuffing, onion, celery and parsley. In a small bowl, beat the eggs; stir in broth and butter. Pour over stuffing mixture. Sprinkle with seasoned salt and pepper; stir well. Pound steak to 1/2-in. thickness. Spread 1 1/2 cups stuffing mixture over steak. Roll up, starting with a short side; tie with string.

2 Place in a 5-qt. slow cooker. Remaining stuffing can be wrapped tightly in foil and placed over the rolled steak. Cover and cook on low for 6-8 hours or until a meat thermometer inserted in stuffing reads 165°. Remove string before slicing

YIELD: 6 SERVINGS.

EDITOR'S NOTE: No liquid is added to the slow cooker. The moisture comes from the meat.

Diane Hixon, Niceville, Florida

This elegant meal is worthy of company. The tender steak cuts easily into appetizing spirals for serving, and extra stuffing cooks conveniently in a foil packet on top of the steak.

beef in mushroom gravy

COOK TIME: 7 TO 8 HOURS

- 2 to 2½ pounds boneless round steak
- 1 to 2 envelopes dry onion soup mix
- 1 can (10¾ ounces) condensed cream of mushroom soup, undiluted
- ½ cup water

Mashed potatoes, optional

Cut steak into six serving-size pieces; place in a slow cooker. Combine soup mix, soup and water; pour over beef. Cover and cook on low for 7-8 hours or until meat is tender. Serve with mashed potatoes if desired.

YIELD: 6 SERVINGS.

Margery Bryan, Royal City, Washington

This is one of the best and easiest meals I've ever made. It has only four ingredients. The meat is nicely seasoned and makes its own gravy.

slow cooker enchiladas

Mary Luebbert, Benton, Kansas

For an easy meal, I rely on this handy recipe. I layer enchilada ingredients in the slow cooker, turn it on and forget about it. With a bit of spice, these hearty enchiladas are especially nice during the colder months.

COOK TIME: 5 TO 7 HOURS

- 1 pound ground beef
- 1 cup chopped onion
- 1/2 cup chopped green pepper
- 1 can (16 ounces) pinto *or* kidney beans, rinsed and drained
- 1 can (15 ounces) black beans, rinsed and drained
- 1 can (10 ounces) diced tomatoes and green chilies, undrained
- 1/3 cup water
- 1 teaspoon chili powder
- 1/2 teaspoon ground cumin
- 1/2 teaspoon salt
- 1/4 teaspoon pepper
- 1 cup (4 ounces) shredded sharp cheddar cheese
- 1 cup (4 ounces) shredded Monterey Jack cheese
- 6 flour tortillas (6 *or* 7 inches)

1 In a skillet, cook beef, onion and green pepper over medium heat until beef is no longer pink and vegetables are tender; drain. Add the next eight ingredients; bring to a boil. Reduce heat; cover and simmer for 10 minutes.

2 Combine cheeses. In a 5-qt. slow cooker, layer about 3/4 cup beef mixture, one tortilla and about 1/3 cup cheese. Repeat layers. Cover and cook on low for 5-7 hours or until heated through.

YIELD: 4 SERVINGS.

slow-cooked meat loaf

COOK TIME: 8 TO 9 HOURS

- 1 egg
- ¼ cup milk
- 2 slices day-old bread, cubed
- ¼ cup finely chopped onion
- 2 tablespoons finely chopped green pepper
- 1 teaspoon salt
- ¼ teaspoon pepper
- 1½ pounds lean ground beef
- ¼ cup ketchup
- 8 medium carrots, cut into 1-inch chunks
- 8 small red potatoes

1 In a bowl, beat egg and milk. Stir in the bread cubes, onion, green pepper, salt and pepper. Add the beef and mix well. Shape into a round loaf. Place in a 5-qt. slow cooker. Spread ketchup on top of loaf. Arrange carrots around loaf. Peel a strip around the center of each potato; place potatoes over carrots.

2 Cover and cook on high for 1 hour. Reduce heat to low; cover and cook 7-8 hours longer or until meat is no longer pink and the vegetables are tender.

YIELD: 4 SERVINGS.

Marna Heitz, Farley, Iowa

What could be more comforting to come home to than moist and tender homemade meat loaf? This one retains its shape in the slow cooker and slices beautifully. Because the vegetables cook with the meat, the entire dinner is ready at the same time.

beef and beans

COOK TIME: 6½ TO 8½ HOURS

1½ **pounds boneless round steak**

1 **tablespoon prepared mustard**

1 **tablespoon chili powder**

½ **teaspoon salt**

¼ **teaspoon pepper**

1 **garlic clove, minced**

2 **cans (14½ ounces *each*) diced tomatoes, undrained**

1 **medium onion, chopped**

1 **beef bouillon cube, crushed**

1 **can (16 ounces) kidney beans, rinsed and drained**

Hot cooked rice

1 Cut steak into thin strips. Combine mustard, chili powder, salt, pepper and garlic in a bowl; add steak and toss to coat. Transfer to a slow cooker; add tomatoes, onion and bouillon.

2 Cover and cook on low for 6-8 hours. Stir in beans; cook 30 minutes longer. Serve over rice.

YIELD: 8 SERVINGS.

Marie Leadmon, Bethesda, Maryland

This deliciously spicy steak and beans over rice will have family and friends asking for more. It's a favorite in my recipe collection because it's so simple and so good.

round steak roll-ups

Kimberly Alonge, Westfield, New York

Since I'm a working mom, I like to assemble these tasty steak rolls the night before and pop them in the slow cooker the next morning before we're all out the door. They make a great meal after a long day.

COOK TIME: 6 HOURS

2 pounds boneless beef round steak

½ cup grated carrot

⅓ cup chopped zucchini

¼ cup chopped sweet red pepper

¼ cup chopped green pepper

¼ cup sliced green onions

2 tablespoons grated Parmesan cheese

1 tablespoon minced fresh parsley *or* 1 teaspoon dried parsley flakes

1 garlic clove, minced

¼ teaspoon salt

¼ teaspoon pepper

2 tablespoons canola oil

1 jar (14 ounces) meatless spaghetti sauce

Hot cooked spaghetti

Additional Parmesan cheese, optional

1 Cut meat into six pieces; pound to ¼-in. thickness. Combine the vegetables, Parmesan cheese and seasonings; place ⅓ cup in the center of each piece. Roll meat up around filling; secure with toothpicks.

2 In a large skillet, brown roll-ups in oil over medium-high heat. Transfer to a 5-qt. slow cooker; top with spaghetti sauce. Cover and cook on low for 6 hours or until meat is tender. Discard toothpicks. Serve roll-ups and sauce over spaghetti. Sprinkle with the additional Parmesan if desired.

YIELD: 6 SERVINGS.

meatball cabbage rolls

COOK TIME: 8 HOURS

- 1 large head cabbage, cored
- 2 cans (one 8 ounces, one 15 ounces) tomato sauce, *divided*
- 1 small onion, chopped
- 1/3 cup uncooked long grain rice
- 2 tablespoons chili powder

Salt and garlic powder to taste

- 1 pound ground beef

1 In a Dutch oven, cook cabbage in boiling water only until the outer leaves fall off head, about 3 minutes. Remove cabbage from water and remove as many leaves as will come off easily. Reserve 14-16 large leaves for rolls. Return cabbage to water if more leaves are needed. Remove the thick vein from each leaf.

2 In a bowl, combine 8 oz. of tomato sauce, onion, rice, chili powder, salt and garlic powder. Crumble beef over mixture; mix well. Shape into 2-in. balls. Place one meatball on each cabbage leaf; fold in sides. Starting at an unfolded edge, roll up leaf to completely enclose meatball. Secure with toothpicks.

3 Place in a 5-qt. slow cooker. Pour remaining tomato sauce over cabbage rolls. Cover and cook on low for 8 hours or until meat is no longer pink and cabbage is tender. Discard toothpicks.

YIELD: 4-6 SERVINGS.

Betty Buckmaster, Muskogee, Oklahoma

My mother would often have these cabbage rolls simmering in her slow cooker when my family and I arrived at her house for weekend visits. The mouth-watering meatballs tucked inside make these stand out from any other cabbage rolls I've tried.

slow-cooked coffee pot roast

COOK TIME: 9½ TO 10½ HOURS

- 2 medium onions, thinly sliced
- 2 garlic cloves, minced
- 1 boneless beef chuck roast (3½ to 4 pounds), quartered
- 1 cup brewed coffee
- ¼ cup soy sauce
- ¼ cup cornstarch
- 6 tablespoons cold water

Place half of onions in a 5-qt. slow cooker. Top with garlic and half of beef. Top with remaining onion and beef. Combine coffee and soy sauce; pour over beef. Cover; cook on low 9-10 hours or until meat is tender. Combine cornstarch and water until smooth; stir into cooking juices. Cover; cook on high 30 minutes or until gravy is thickened.

YIELD: 10-12 SERVINGS.

Janet Dominick, Bagley, Minnesota

As a working wife and mother, I don't have much time to fix meals. I spend a few minutes in the morning on this entree, and it tastes like I spent hours at it.

slow cooker lasagna

Lisa Micheletti, Collierville, Tennessee

Convenient no-cook lasagna noodles take the work out of this traditional favorite adapted for the slow cooker. Because it's so easy to assemble, it's great for work days as well as weekends. We like it accompanied by garlic bread or Parmesan cheese toast.

COOK TIME: 4 TO 5 HOURS

- 1 pound ground beef
- 1 large onion, chopped
- 2 garlic cloves, minced
- 1 can (29 ounces) tomato sauce
- 1 cup water
- 1 can (6 ounces) tomato paste
- 1 teaspoon salt
- 1 teaspoon dried oregano
- 1 package (8 ounces) no-cook lasagna noodles
- 4 cups (16 ounces) shredded part-skim mozzarella cheese
- 1½ cups (12 ounces) small-curd cottage cheese
- ½ cup grated Parmesan cheese

1 In a skillet, cook beef, onion and garlic over medium heat until meat is no longer pink; drain. Add the tomato sauce, water, tomato paste, salt and oregano; mix well. Spread a fourth of the meat sauce in an ungreased 5-qt. slow cooker. Arrange a third of the noodles over sauce (break noodles if necessary).

2 Combine the cheeses; spoon a third of the mixture over noodles. Repeat layers twice. Top with remaining meat sauce. Cover; cook on low for 4-5 hours or until noodles are tender.

YIELD: 6-8 SERVINGS.

slow-cooked rump roast

COOK TIME: 10½ TO 11½ HOURS

- 1 boneless beef rump roast
  (3 to 3½ pounds)
- 2 tablespoons vegetable oil
- 4 medium carrots, halved lengthwise
  and cut into 2-inch pieces
- 3 medium potatoes, peeled and cut
  into chunks
- 2 small onions, sliced
- ½ cup water
- 6 to 8 tablespoons horseradish
- ¼ cup red wine vinegar
- ¼ cup Worcestershire sauce
- 2 garlic cloves, minced
- 1½ to 2 teaspoons celery salt
- 3 tablespoons cornstarch
- ⅓ cup cold water

1 Cut roast in half. In a large skillet, brown meat on all sides in oil over medium-high heat; drain. Place carrots and potatoes in a 5-qt. slow cooker. Top with meat and onions. Combine the water, horseradish, vinegar, Worcestershire sauce, garlic and celery salt. Pour over meat. Cover and cook on low for 10-11 hours or until meat and vegetables are tender.

2 Combine cornstarch and cold water until smooth; stir into slow cooker. Cover and cook on high for 30 minutes or until gravy is thickened.

YIELD: 6-8 SERVINGS.

Mimi Walker, Palmyra, Pennsylvania

Cooking pot roast in horseradish sauce in the slow cooker is a tasty new twist. It gives a tangy flavor, tender vegetables and great gravy that even young kids enjoy.

throw-together short ribs

COOK TIME: 4 TO 5 HOURS

⅓ cup water

¼ cup tomato paste

3 tablespoons brown sugar

1 tablespoon prepared mustard

2 teaspoons seasoned salt

2 teaspoons cider vinegar

1 teaspoon Worcestershire sauce

1 teaspoon beef bouillon granules

2 pounds beef short ribs

1 small tomato, chopped

1 small onion, chopped

1 tablespoon cornstarch

1 tablespoon cold water

1 In a 3-qt. slow cooker, combine the first eight ingredients. Add the ribs, tomato and onion. Cover and cook on low for 4-5 hours or until meat is tender.

2 In a small bowl, combine cornstarch and cold water until smooth; gradually stir into cooking juices. Cover and cook for 10-15 minutes or until thickened.

YIELD: 4-5 SERVINGS.

Lamya Asiff, Delburne, Alberta

This recipe takes no time to prepare and results in the most delicious, fall-off-the-bone short ribs. The longer you cook them, the better they get!

hearty new england dinner

Claire McCombs, San Diego, California

This favorite slow-cooker recipe came from a friend. At first, my husband was a bit skeptical about a roast that wasn't fixed in the oven, but he loves the old-fashioned goodness of this version. The horseradish in the gravy adds zip.

COOK TIME: 7½ TO 9½ HOURS

- 2 medium carrots, sliced
- 1 medium onion, sliced
- 1 celery rib, sliced
- 1 boneless chuck roast (about 3 pounds)
- 1 teaspoon salt, *divided*
- ¼ teaspoon pepper
- 1 envelope onion soup mix
- 2 cups water
- 1 tablespoon vinegar
- 1 bay leaf
- ½ small head cabbage, cut into wedges
- 3 tablespoons butter
- 2 tablespoons all-purpose flour
- 1 tablespoon dried minced onion
- 2 tablespoons prepared horseradish

1 Place carrots, onion and celery in a 5-qt. slow cooker. Place the roast on top; sprinkle with ½ teaspoon salt and pepper. Add soup mix, water, vinegar and bay leaf. Cover and cook on low for 7-9 hours or until beef is tender.

2 Remove beef and keep warm; discard bay leaf. Add cabbage. Cover and cook on high for 30-40 minutes or until cabbage is tender.

3 Meanwhile, melt butter in a small saucepan; stir in flour and onion. Add 1½ cups cooking liquid from the slow cooker. Stir in horseradish and remaining salt; bring to a boil.

4 Cook and stir over low heat until thick and smooth, about 2 minutes. Serve with roast and vegetables.

YIELD: 6-8 SERVINGS.

slow-cooked swiss steak

COOK TIME: 8 TO 9 HOURS

- ¾ cup all-purpose flour
- 1 teaspoon pepper
- ¼ teaspoon salt
- 2 to 2½ pounds boneless round steak
- 1 to 2 tablespoons butter
- 1 can (10¾ ounces) condensed cream of mushroom soup, undiluted
- 1⅓ cups water
- 1 cup sliced celery, optional
- ½ cup chopped onion
- 1 garlic clove, minced
- 1 to 3 teaspoons beef bouillon granules

In a shallow bowl, combine flour, pepper and salt. Cut steak into six serving-size pieces; dredge in flour mixture. In a skillet, brown steak in butter. Transfer to a slow cooker. Combine the remaining ingredients; pour over steak. Cover and cook on low for 8-9 hours or until the meat is tender.

YIELD: 6 SERVINGS.

Kathie Morris, Redmond, Oregon

Everyone raves about how tender and rich-tasting this dish is. Leftovers from a double batch make super Stroganoff the next night. I crumble the meat and mix it with the gravy, plus sour cream and Worcestershire sauce.

meaty spaghetti sauce

COOK TIME: 8 HOURS

- 1 **pound ground beef**
- 1 **pound bulk Italian sausage**
- 1 **medium green pepper, chopped**
- 1 **medium onion, chopped**
- 8 **garlic cloves, minced**
- 3 **cans (14½ ounces *each*) Italian diced tomatoes, drained**
- 2 **cans (15 ounces *each*) tomato sauce**
- 2 **cans (6 ounces *each*) tomato paste**
- ⅓ **cup sugar**
- 2 **tablespoons Italian seasoning**
- 1 **tablespoon dried basil**
- 2 **teaspoons dried marjoram**
- 1 **teaspoon salt**
- ½ **teaspoon pepper**

Hot cooked spaghetti

In a large skillet over medium heat, cook beef and sausage until no longer pink; drain. Transfer to a 5-qt. slow cooker. Stir in green pepper, onion, garlic, tomatoes, tomato sauce, paste, sugar and seasonings; mix well. Cover and cook on low for 8 hours or until bubbly. Serve over spaghetti.

YIELD: 12 SERVINGS.

Arlene Sommers, Redmond, Washington

My family always enjoyed my homemade spaghetti sauce, but it's so time-consuming to make on the stovetop. My busy grown daughter adapted my recipe to take advantage of her slow cooker. The flavorful sauce still receives compliments.

easy chow mein

Kay Bade, Mitchell, South Dakota

Our daughter welcomed me home from a hospital stay some years ago with this Oriental dish and a copy of the recipe. Now that I'm a widow, I freeze leftovers for fast future meals.

COOK TIME: 4 HOURS

1 pound ground beef

1 medium onion, chopped

1 bunch celery, sliced

2 cans (14 ounces *each*) Chinese vegetables, drained

2 envelopes brown gravy mix

2 tablespoons soy sauce

Hot cooked rice

1 In a skillet, cook beef and onion over medium heat until meat is no longer pink; drain. Transfer to a slow cooker. Stir in the celery, Chinese vegetables, gravy mixes and soy sauce.

2 Cover and cook on low for 4 hours or until celery is tender, stirring occasionally. Serve over rice.

YIELD: 8 SERVINGS.

it's best to brown

For the best color and flavor, ground beef should be browned before using it in a slow cooker recipe. The exception is when preparing a meat loaf or similar dish.

Although it's not necessary to brown other cuts of meat or poultry, the process can enhance the flavor and appearance and reduce the fat in the finished dish.

slow-cooked tamale casserole

COOK TIME: 4 HOURS

- 1 pound ground beef
- 1 egg
- 1½ cups milk
- ¾ cup cornmeal
- 1 can (15¼ ounces) whole kernel corn, drained
- 1 can (14½ ounces) diced tomatoes, undrained
- 1 can (2¼ ounces) sliced ripe olives, drained
- 1 envelope chili seasoning
- 1 teaspoon seasoned salt
- 1 cup (4 ounces) shredded cheddar cheese

1 In a skillet, cook beef over medium heat until no longer pink; drain. In a bowl, combine the egg, milk and cornmeal until smooth. Add corn, tomatoes, olives, chili seasoning, seasoned salt and beef. Transfer to a greased slow cooker.

2 Cover and cook on high for 3 hours and 45 minutes. Sprinkle with cheese; cover and cook 15 minutes longer or until cheese is melted.

YIELD: 6 SERVINGS.

Diana Briggs, Veneta, Oregon

I've been making this recipe for years because my family really likes it. It's great for busy days, since you assemble it earlier in the day and let it cook.

cube steaks with gravy

COOK TIME: 8½ HOURS

⅓ cup all-purpose flour

6 beef cube steaks (1½ pounds)

1 tablespoon vegetable oil

1 large onion, sliced and separated into rings

3 cups water, *divided*

1 envelope brown gravy mix

1 envelope mushroom gravy mix

1 envelope onion gravy mix

Hot mashed potatoes *or* cooked noodles

1 Place flour in a large resealable plastic bag. Add steaks, a few at a time, and shake until completely coated. In a skillet, cook steaks in oil until lightly browned on each side. Transfer to a slow cooker. Add the onion and 2 cups water. Cover and cook on low for 8 hours or until meat is tender.

2 In a bowl, whisk together gravy mixes with remaining water. Add to slow cooker; cook 30 minutes longer. Serve over mashed potatoes or noodles.

YIELD: 6 SERVINGS.

Judy Long, Limestone, Tennessee

With this recipe, good flavor doesn't take a back seat to convenience. Cube steaks can be tough and chewy. But fixed this way, they're a tender and tasty family favorite.

saucy italian roast

Jan Roat, Grass Range, Montana

This tender roast is one of my favorite fix-it-and-forget-it meals. I thicken the juices with a little flour and add ketchup, then serve the sauce and beef slices over pasta. It's deliciously different.

COOK TIME: 8 TO 9 HOURS

- 1 boneless rump roast (3 to 3½ pounds)
- ½ to 1 teaspoon salt
- ½ teaspoon garlic powder
- ¼ teaspoon pepper
- 1 jar (4½ ounces) sliced mushrooms, drained
- 1 medium onion, diced
- 1 jar (14 ounces) spaghetti sauce
- ¼ to ½ cup red wine *or* beef broth

Hot cooked pasta

Cut the roast in half. Combine salt, garlic powder and pepper; rub over roast. Place in a 5-qt. slow cooker. Top with mushrooms and onion. Combine the spaghetti sauce and wine or broth; pour over meat and vegetables. Cover and cook on low for 8-9 hours or until meat is tender. Slice roast; serve over pasta with pan juices.

YIELD: 8-10 SERVINGS.

try to trim down

When preparing meat or poultry for the slow cooker, trim off excess fat. It retains heat, and large amounts of fat could raise the temperature of the cooking liquid, causing the meat to overcook.

spiced pot roast

COOK TIME: 8 TO 9 HOURS

- 1 boneless beef chuck roast (about 2½ pounds)
- 1 medium onion, chopped
- 1 can (14½ ounces) diced tomatoes, undrained
- ¼ cup white vinegar
- 3 tablespoons tomato puree
- 2 teaspoons Dijon mustard
- ½ teaspoon lemon juice
- 4½ teaspoons poppy seeds
- 2 garlic cloves, minced
- 2¼ teaspoons sugar
- ½ teaspoon ground ginger
- ½ teaspoon salt
- ½ teaspoon dried rosemary, crushed
- ¼ teaspoon ground turmeric
- ¼ teaspoon ground cumin
- ¼ teaspoon crushed red pepper flakes
- ⅛ teaspoon ground cloves
- 1 bay leaf
- Hot cooked noodles

1 Place roast in a slow cooker. In a large bowl, combine the onion, tomatoes, vinegar, tomato puree, mustard, lemon juice and seasonings; pour over roast.

2 Cover and cook on low for 8-9 hours or until meat is tender. Discard bay leaf. Thicken cooking juices if desired. Serve over noodles.

YIELD: 6-8 SERVINGS.

Loren Martin, Big Cabin, Oklahoma

Just pour these ingredients over your pot roast and let the slow cooker do the work. Herbs and spices give the beef an excellent taste. I often serve this roast over noodles or with mashed potatoes, using the juices as a gravy.

slow-cooked sirloin

COOK TIME: 3½ TO 4½ HOURS

1 boneless beef sirloin steak
(1½ pounds)

1 medium onion, cut into 1-inch chunks

1 medium green pepper, cut into
1-inch chunks

1 can (14½ ounces) reduced-sodium
beef broth

¼ cup Worcestershire sauce

¼ teaspoon dill weed

¼ teaspoon dried thyme

¼ teaspoon pepper

Dash crushed red pepper flakes

2 tablespoons cornstarch

2 tablespoons water

1 In a large nonstick skillet coated with nonstick cooking spray, brown beef on both sides. Place onion and green pepper in a 3-qt. slow cooker. Top with beef. Combine the broth, Worcestershire sauce, dill, thyme, pepper and pepper flakes; pour over beef. Cover and cook on high for 3-4 hours or until meat reaches desired doneness and vegetables are crisp-tender.

2 Remove beef and keep warm. Combine cornstarch and water until smooth; gradually stir into cooking juices. Cover and cook about 30 minutes longer or until slightly thickened. Return beef to the slow cooker; heat through.

YIELD: 6 SERVINGS.

Vicki Tormaschy, Dickinson, North Dakota

My family of five likes to eat beef, so this recipe is a favorite. I usually serve it with homemade bread or rolls to soak up the tasty gravy.

corned beef and cabbage

Karen Waters, Laurel, Maryland

I first tried this fuss-free way to cook traditional corned beef and cabbage for St. Patrick's Day a few years ago. Now it's a regular in my menu planning. This is terrific with Dijon mustard and crusty bread.

COOK TIME: 8 TO 9 HOURS

- 1 medium onion, cut into wedges
- 4 medium potatoes, peeled and quartered
- 1 pound baby carrots
- 3 cups water
- 3 garlic cloves, minced
- 1 bay leaf
- 2 tablespoons sugar
- 2 tablespoons cider vinegar
- 1/2 teaspoon pepper
- 1 corned beef brisket with spice packet (2 1/2 to 3 pounds), cut in half
- 1 small head cabbage, cut into wedges

Place the onion, potatoes and carrots in a 5-qt. slow cooker. Combine water, garlic, bay leaf, sugar, vinegar, pepper and contents of spice packet; pour over vegetables. Top with brisket and cabbage. Cover and cook on low for 8-9 hours or until meat and vegetables are tender. Remove bay leaf before serving.

YIELD: 6-8 SERVINGS.

spread it out

For meats to cook evenly in the slow cooker, allow some space between the pieces, so the heat can circulate and the seasonings can be nicely distributed.

slow-cooked pepper steak

COOK TIME: 6 TO 7 HOURS

1½ to 2 pounds beef round steak

2 tablespoons vegetable oil

¼ cup soy sauce

1 cup chopped onion

1 garlic clove, minced

1 teaspoon sugar

½ teaspoon salt

¼ teaspoon pepper

¼ teaspoon ground ginger

4 tomatoes, cut into eighths *or* 1 can (14½ ounces) diced tomatoes, undrained

2 large green peppers, cut into strips

½ cup cold water

1 tablespoon cornstarch

Hot cooked noodles *or* rice

Sue Gronholz, Columbus, Wisconsin

After a long day in our greenhouse raising bedding plants for sale, I appreciate coming in to this hearty beef dish for supper.

Cut beef into 3-in. x 1-in. strips; brown in oil in a skillet. Transfer to a slow cooker. Combine the next seven ingredients; pour over beef. Cover and cook on low for 5-6 hours or until meat is tender. Add tomatoes and green peppers; cook on low for 1 hour longer. Combine the cold water and cornstarch to make a paste; stir into liquid in slow cooker and cook on high until thickened. Serve over noodles or rice.

YIELD: 6-8 SERVINGS.

apple & onion beef pot roast

COOK TIME: 5 TO 6 HOURS

1 boneless beef sirloin tip roast (3 pounds), cut in half

1 cup water

1 teaspoon seasoned salt

½ teaspoon reduced-sodium soy sauce

½ teaspoon Worcestershire sauce

¼ teaspoon garlic powder

1 large tart apple, quartered

1 large onion, sliced

2 tablespoons cornstarch

2 tablespoons cold water

⅛ teaspoon browning sauce

1 In a large nonstick skillet coated with nonstick cooking spray, brown roast on all sides. Transfer to a 5-qt. slow cooker. Add water to the skillet, stirring to loosen any browned bits; pour over roast. Sprinkle with seasoned salt, soy sauce, Worcestershire sauce and garlic powder. Top with apple and onion. Cover and cook on low for 5-6 hours or until the meat is tender.

2 Remove roast and onion; let stand for 15 minutes before slicing. Strain cooking liquid into a saucepan, discarding apple. Bring liquid to a boil; cook until reduced to 2 cups, about 15 minutes. Combine cornstarch and cold water until smooth; stir in browning sauce. Stir into cooking liquid. Bring to a boil; cook and stir for 2 minutes or until thickened. Serve over beef and onion.

YIELD: 8 SERVINGS.

Rachel Koistinen, Hayti, South Dakota

Rely on your slow cooker to help prepare this moist pot roast. I thicken the juices to make a pleasing apple gravy that's wonderful over the beef slices and onions.

two-step stroganoff

Roberta Menefee, Walcott, New York

I especially like to use my slow cooker on hot summer days when I want to keep my kitchen cool. I'm always trying new recipes for different occasions.

COOK TIME: 7 HOURS

2 pounds ground beef, cooked and drained

2 medium onions, chopped

1 cup beef consomme

1 can (4 ounces) mushroom stems and pieces, drained

3 tablespoons tomato paste

2 garlic cloves, minced

1½ teaspoons salt

¼ teaspoon pepper

2 tablespoons all-purpose flour

¾ cup sour cream

¼ cup minced fresh parsley, optional

Hot cooked noodles

1 In a 3-qt. slow cooker, combine the first eight ingredients; mix well. Cover and cook on low for 6 hours.

2 In a small bowl, combine flour and sour cream until smooth; stir into beef mixture. Cover and cook 1 hour longer or until thickened. Garnish with parsley if desired. Serve over noodles.

YIELD: 6 SERVINGS.

beefy au gratin potatoes

COOK TIME: 4 HOURS

1 package (5¼ ounces) au gratin *or* cheddar and bacon potatoes

1 can (15¼ ounces) whole kernel corn, drained

1 can (10¾ ounces) condensed cream of potato soup, undiluted

1 cup water

1 can (4 ounces) chopped green chilies, drained

1 can (4 ounces) mushroom stems and pieces, drained

1 jar (4 ounces) diced pimientos, drained

1 pound ground beef

1 medium onion, chopped

1 Set potato sauce mix aside. Place potatoes in a slow cooker; top with corn. In a bowl, combine the soup, water, chilies, mushrooms, pimientos and reserved sauce mix; mix well. Pour a third of the mixture over corn.

2 In a skillet, cook beef and onion over medium heat until the meat is no longer pink; drain. Transfer to slow cooker. Top with the remaining sauce mixture. Do not stir. Cover and cook on low for 4 hours or until potatoes are tender.

YIELD: 4-6 SERVINGS.

Eileen Majerus, Pine Island, Minnesota

It's easy to vary the flavor of this hearty, family-favorite casserole by using different kinds of soup and potato mixes. We enjoy the comforting combination of beef, potatoes and vegetables in this dish. I usually serve up heaping helpings with a salad and garlic bread.

chicken & turkey

148

176

From moist, mouth-watering Chicken Cacciatore (p. 148) to spiced-up Turkey Enchiladas (p. 176), you can take your pick of the best family-favorite poultry recipes created for the slow cooker. Everyone's a guaranteed winner with your family, too!

Covered cooking in your countertop appliance means juicier chicken and turkey…and more mealtime compliments for you! Because most of these recipes use just one crock for prep and cooking, cleanup is a breeze, even on the busiest days.

rosemary cashew chicken

COOK TIME: 4 TO 5 HOURS

1 broiler/fryer chicken (3 to 4 pounds), cut up and skin removed

1 medium onion, thinly sliced

1/3 cup orange juice concentrate

1 teaspoon dried rosemary, crushed

1 teaspoon salt

1/4 teaspoon cayenne pepper

2 tablespoons all-purpose flour

3 tablespoons water

1/4 to 1/2 cup chopped cashews

Hot cooked pasta

1 Place chicken in a slow cooker. Combine onion, orange juice concentrate, rosemary, salt and cayenne; pour over chicken. Cover and cook on low for 4-5 hours or until chicken juices run clear. Remove the chicken and keep warm.

2 In a saucepan, combine flour and water until smooth. Stir in cooking juices. Bring to a boil; cook and stir for 2 minutes or until thickened. Stir in cashews. Pour over chicken. Serve with pasta.

YIELD: 4-6 SERVINGS.

Ruth Andrewson, Peck, Idaho

This elegant entree with delicious herb flavor is mouth-watering. Cashews add richness and crunch.

no-fuss chicken

COOK TIME: 2 TO 2½ HOURS

- ⅔ cup all-purpose flour
- 1 teaspoon dried sage
- 1 teaspoon dried basil
- 1 teaspoon seasoned salt
- 1 broiler/fryer chicken (2½ to 3 pounds), cut up
- ¼ cup butter
- 2 cups chicken broth

1 In a shallow bowl, combine flour, sage, basil and seasoned salt; coat chicken. Reserve remaining flour mixture. In a large skillet, melt butter; brown chicken on all sides. Transfer to a slow cooker.

2 Add ¼ cup reserved flour mixture to the skillet (discarding the rest); stir until smooth. When mixture begins to bubble, stir in chicken broth and bring to a boil; boil for 1 minute. Pour over chicken. Cover and cook on high for 2 to 2½ hours or until chicken juices run clear.

YIELD: 4 SERVINGS.

Sandra Flick, Toledo, Ohio

My mother-in-law devised this recipe when her children were growing up. It was a favorite Sunday dish because it could cook while the family was at church. When they came home, it didn't take long to put dinner on the table.

chicken cacciatore

Aggie Arnold-Norman, Liberty, Pennsylvania

My husband and I milk 125 cows. There are days when there's just no time left for cooking! It's really nice to be able to come in from the barn at night and smell this meal simmering—dinner is a simple matter of dishing it up.

COOK TIME: 6 TO 8 HOURS

- 2 medium onions, thinly sliced
- 1 broiler/fryer chicken (2½ to 3 pounds), cut up and skin removed
- 2 garlic cloves, minced
- 1 teaspoon salt
- ¼ teaspoon pepper
- 1 to 2 teaspoons dried oregano
- ½ teaspoon dried basil
- 1 bay leaf
- 1 can (14½ ounces) diced tomatoes
- 1 can (8 ounces) tomato sauce
- 1 can (4 ounces) mushroom stems and pieces *or* 1 cup fresh mushrooms
- ¼ cup dry white wine *or* water

  Hot cooked pasta

1 Place sliced onions in bottom of slow cooker. Add the chicken, seasonings, tomatoes, sauce, mushrooms and wine or water.

2 Cover and cook on low for 6-8 hours. Discard bay leaf. Serve chicken with sauce over pasta.

YIELD: 6 SERVINGS.

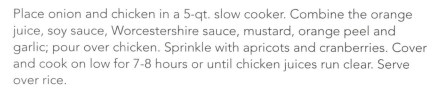

fruited chicken

COOK TIME: 7 TO 8 HOURS

- 1 large onion, sliced
- 6 boneless skinless chicken breast halves
- 1/3 cup orange juice
- 2 tablespoons soy sauce
- 2 tablespoons Worcestershire sauce
- 2 tablespoons Dijon mustard
- 1 tablespoon grated orange peel
- 2 garlic cloves, minced
- 1/2 cup chopped dried apricots
- 1/2 cup dried cranberries

Hot cooked rice

Place onion and chicken in a 5-qt. slow cooker. Combine the orange juice, soy sauce, Worcestershire sauce, mustard, orange peel and garlic; pour over chicken. Sprinkle with apricots and cranberries. Cover and cook on low for 7-8 hours or until chicken juices run clear. Serve over rice.

YIELD: 6 SERVINGS.

Mirien Church, Aurora, Colorado

The combination of fruity flavors in this easy chicken dish is unique and tasty. My husband loves having hot home-cooked meals each night…and this particular one is always a hit!

tender barbecued chicken

COOK TIME: 8 TO 10 HOURS

1 broiler/fryer chicken (3 to 4 pounds), cut up

1 medium onion, thinly sliced

1 medium lemon, thinly sliced

1 bottle (18 ounces) barbecue sauce

¾ cup regular cola

Place chicken in a slow cooker. Top with onion and lemon slices. Combine barbecue sauce and cola; pour over all. Cover and cook on low for 8-10 hours or until the chicken juices run clear.

YIELD: 4-6 SERVINGS.

EDITOR'S NOTE: This recipe was tested with K.C. Masterpiece brand barbecue sauce.

Jacqueline Blanton, Gaffney, South Carolina

I'm a teacher and work most of the day, so slow-cooked meals are a great help. One of my family's favorites is this moist chicken. For an appealing look, choose a darker brown barbecue sauce.

chicken in a pot

COOK TIME: 7 TO 9 HOURS

3 medium carrots, cut into ¾-inch pieces

2 celery ribs with leaves, cut into ¾-inch pieces

2 medium onions, sliced

1 broiler/fryer chicken (3 to 4 pounds), cut up

½ cup chicken broth

1½ teaspoons salt

1 teaspoon dried basil

½ teaspoon pepper

In a 5-qt. slow cooker, place carrots, celery ribs and onions. Top with chicken. Combine remaining ingredients; pour over the chicken. Cover and cook on low for 7-9 hours or until chicken juices run clear and vegetables are tender. Serve with a slotted spoon.

YIELD: 6 SERVINGS.

Alpha Wilson, Roswell, New Mexico

It takes just minutes to get this satisfying supper ready for the slow cooker. And at the end of a busy day, your family will appreciate the simple goodness of tender chicken and vegetables. It's one of our favorite meals.

sage turkey thighs

Natalie Swanson, Catonsville, Maryland

I created this for my boys, who love dark meat. It's more convenient than cooking a whole turkey. It reminds me of our traditional Thanksgiving turkey and stuffing seasoned with sage.

COOK TIME: 6 TO 8 HOURS

- 4 medium carrots, halved
- 1 medium onion, chopped
- ½ cup water
- 2 garlic cloves, minced
- 1½ teaspoons rubbed sage, *divided*
- 2 turkey thighs *or* drumsticks (about 2 pounds), skin removed
- 1 teaspoon browning sauce, optional
- ¼ teaspoon salt
- ⅛ teaspoon pepper
- 1 tablespoon cornstarch
- ¼ cup cold water

1 In a slow cooker, combine the carrots, onion, water, garlic and 1 teaspoon sage. Top with turkey. Sprinkle with the remaining sage. Cover and cook on low for 6-8 hours or until a meat thermometer reads 180°.

2 Remove turkey and keep warm. Skim fat from cooking juices; strain and reserve vegetables. Place vegetables in a food processor; cover and process until smooth. Place in a saucepan; add cooking juices. Bring to a boil. Add browning sauce if desired, salt and pepper.

3 Combine the cornstarch and water until smooth; add to the juices. Bring to a boil; cook and stir for 2 minutes or until thickened. Serve with the turkey.

YIELD: 4 SERVINGS.

golden chicken and noodles

COOK TIME: 6 TO 7 HOURS

- 6 boneless skinless chicken breast halves (1½ pounds)
- 2 cans (10¾ ounces *each*) condensed broccoli cheese soup, undiluted
- 2 cups milk
- 1 small onion, chopped
- ½ to 1 teaspoon salt
- ½ to 1 teaspoon dried basil
- ⅛ teaspoon pepper

Hot cooked noodles

Cut chicken pieces in half; place in a 5-qt. slow cooker. Combine the soup, milk, onion, salt, basil and pepper; pour over chicken. Cover and cook on high for 1 hour. Reduce heat to low; cover and cook 5-6 hours longer or until meat juices run clear. Serve over noodles.

YIELD: 6 SERVINGS.

Charlotte McDaniel, Anniston, Alabama

This tender chicken cooks up in a golden sauce that is nicely flavored with basil. It's great for taking to a potluck supper, especially if you work and don't have time to cook during the day.

sweet and tangy chicken

COOK TIME: 8 TO 9 HOURS

- 8 boneless skinless chicken breast halves
- 2 bottles (18 ounces *each*) barbecue sauce
- 1 can (20 ounces) pineapple chunks, undrained
- 1 medium green pepper, chopped
- 1 medium onion, chopped
- 2 garlic cloves, minced

Hot cooked rice

1 Place four chicken breasts in a 5-qt. slow cooker. Combine barbecue sauce, pineapple, green pepper, onion and garlic; pour half over the chicken. Top with remaining chicken and sauce.

2 Cover and cook on low for 8-9 hours or until chicken is tender and meat juices run clear. Thicken sauce if desired. Serve the chicken and sauce over rice.

YIELD: 8 SERVINGS.

Mary Zawlocki, Gig Harbor, Washington

Spicy barbecue sauce blends with sweet pineapple in this quick-to-fix chicken dish. It's tasty enough for a company dinner…just add a salad and rolls.

saucy apricot chicken

COOK TIME: 4 TO 5 HOURS

- 6 boneless skinless chicken breast halves (about 1½ pounds)
- 2 jars (12 ounces *each*) apricot preserves
- 1 envelope onion soup mix

Hot cooked rice

Place chicken in a slow cooker. Combine the preserves and soup mix; spoon over chicken. Cover and cook on low for 4-5 hours or until tender. Serve over rice.

YIELD: 6 SERVINGS.

Dee Gray, Kokomo, Indiana

Just four ingredients are all you'll need for a scrumptious chicken entree. The tangy glaze is just as wonderful with ham or turkey.

sunday chicken supper

Ruthann Martin, Louisville, Ohio

This yummy slow-cooked sensation is loaded with chicken, vegetables and seasonings. It's a dish that satisfies the biggest appetites.

COOK TIME: 6 TO 8 HOURS

- 4 medium carrots, cut into 2-inch pieces
- 1 medium onion, chopped
- 1 celery rib, cut into 2-inch pieces
- 2 cups cut fresh green beans (2-inch pieces)
- 5 small red potatoes, quartered
- 2 to 4 tablespoons vegetable oil
- 1 broiler/fryer chicken (3 to 3½ pounds), cut up
- 4 bacon strips, cooked and crumbled
- 1½ cups hot water
- 2 teaspoons chicken bouillon granules
- 1 teaspoon salt
- ½ teaspoon dried thyme
- ½ teaspoon dried basil

Pinch pepper

1 In a 5-qt. slow cooker, layer first five ingredients in order listed. In a skillet, heat oil; brown the chicken on all sides. Transfer to a slow cooker; top with bacon.

2 In a bowl, combine remaining ingredients; pour over top. Do not stir. Cover; cook on low for 6-8 hours or until vegetables are tender and chicken juices run clear. Remove chicken and vegetables.

3 If desired, thicken juices for gravy in a saucepan. Return chicken and vegetables to slow cooker. Drizzle with gravy.

YIELD: 4 SERVINGS.

ham 'n' swiss chicken

COOK TIME: 4 TO 5 HOURS

  2 eggs

  2 cups milk, *divided*

 ½ cup butter, melted

 ½ cup chopped celery

  1 teaspoon finely chopped onion

  8 slices bread, cubed

 12 thin slices deli ham, rolled up

  2 cups (8 ounces) shredded
     Swiss cheese

2½ cups cubed cooked chicken

  1 can (10¾ ounces) condensed
     cream of chicken soup, undiluted

1 In a large bowl, beat the eggs and 1½ cups milk. Add butter, celery and onion. Stir in bread cubes. Place half of the mixture in a greased slow cooker; top with half of the rolled-up ham, cheese and chicken. Combine soup and remaining milk; pour half over the chicken. Repeat layers once.

2 Cover and cook on low for 4-5 hours or until a thermometer inserted into the bread mixture reads 160°.

YIELD: 6 SERVINGS.

Dorothy Witmer, Ephrata, Pennsylvania

This saucy casserole allows you to enjoy all the rich flavor of traditional chicken cordon bleu with less effort. It's a snap to layer the ingredients and let them cook all afternoon. Just toss a salad to make this meal complete.

chicken a la king

COOK TIME: 7½ TO 8½ HOURS

1 can (10¾ ounces) condensed cream of chicken soup, undiluted

3 tablespoons all-purpose flour

¼ teaspoon pepper

Dash cayenne pepper

1 pound boneless skinless chicken breasts, cut into cubes

1 celery rib, chopped

½ cup chopped green pepper

¼ cup chopped onion

1 package (10 ounces) frozen peas, thawed

2 tablespoons diced pimientos, drained

Hot cooked rice

Eleanor Mielke, Snohomish, Washington

When I know I'll be having a busy day with little time for cooking, I prepare this tasty main dish. Brimming with tender chicken and colorful vegetables, it has a tempting aroma while cooking—and tastes even better.

1 In a slow cooker, combine soup, flour, pepper and cayenne until smooth. Stir in chicken, celery, green pepper and onion. Cover and cook on low for 7-8 hours or until meat juices run clear.

2 Stir in peas and pimientos. Cook 30 minutes longer or until heated through. Serve over rice.

YIELD: 6 SERVINGS.

slow-cooked lemon chicken

Walter Powell, Wilmington, Delaware

Garlic, oregano and lemon juice give spark to this memorable main dish. It's easy to prepare—just brown the chicken in a skillet, then let the slow cooker do the work. I'm proud to serve this dish to company.

COOK TIME: 3½ TO 4½ HOURS

- 6 bone-in chicken breast halves (about 3 pounds), skin removed
- 1 teaspoon dried oregano
- ½ teaspoon seasoned salt
- ¼ teaspoon pepper
- 2 tablespoons butter
- ¼ cup water
- 3 tablespoons lemon juice
- 2 garlic cloves, minced
- 1 teaspoon chicken bouillon granules
- 2 teaspoons minced fresh parsley

Hot cooked rice

1 Pat the chicken dry with paper towels. Combine the oregano, seasoned salt and pepper; rub over the chicken. In a skillet over medium heat, brown the chicken in butter; transfer to a 5-qt. slow cooker.

2 Add the water, lemon juice, garlic and bouillon to the skillet; bring to a boil, stirring to loosen browned bits. Pour over chicken. Cover and cook on low for 3-4 hours.

3 Baste the chicken. Add parsley. Cover and cook 15-30 minutes longer or until meat juices run clear. If desired, thicken cooking juices and serve over chicken and rice.

YIELD: 6 SERVINGS.

herbed chicken and veggies

COOK TIME: 8 TO 9 HOURS

- 1 broiler/fryer chicken (3 to 4 pounds), cut up and skin removed
- 2 medium tomatoes, chopped
- 1 medium onion, chopped
- 2 garlic cloves, minced
- $\frac{1}{2}$ cup chicken broth
- 2 tablespoons white wine *or* additional chicken broth
- 1 bay leaf
- 1$\frac{1}{2}$ teaspoons salt
- 1 teaspoon dried thyme
- $\frac{1}{4}$ teaspoon pepper
- 2 cups broccoli florets

Hot cooked rice

1 Place chicken in a slow cooker. Top with tomatoes, onion and garlic. Combine broth, wine or additional broth, bay leaf, salt, thyme and pepper; pour over chicken. Cover and cook on low for 7-8 hours.

2 Add broccoli; cook 45-60 minutes longer or until the chicken juices run clear and the broccoli is tender. Discard bay leaf. Thicken pan juices if desired. Serve over rice.

YIELD: 4-6 SERVINGS.

Dorothy Pritchett, Wills Point, Texas

This subtly seasoned chicken and vegetable combination is a snap to prepare on a hectic working day. A dessert is all that's needed to complete this satisfying supper.

chicken veggie alfredo

COOK TIME: 6 TO 8 HOURS

- 4 boneless skinless chicken breast halves
- 1 tablespoon vegetable oil
- 1 jar (16 ounces) Alfredo sauce
- 1 can (15-1/4 ounces) whole kernel corn, drained
- 1 cup frozen peas, thawed
- 1 jar (4-1/2 ounces) sliced mushrooms, drained
- 1/2 cup chopped onion
- 1/2 cup water
- 1/2 teaspoon garlic salt
- 1/4 teaspoon pepper

Hot cooked linguine

In a large skillet, brown chicken in oil. Transfer to a slow cooker. In a bowl, combine the Alfredo sauce, corn, peas, mushrooms, onion, water, garlic salt and pepper. Pour over chicken. Cover and cook on low for 6-8 hours or until a meat thermometer reads 170°. Serve over linguine.

YIELD: 4 SERVINGS.

Jennifer Jordan, Hubbard, Ohio

My family loves this dinner—it's easy to make and a great way to save time after a busy day. If you like, add other veggies to suit your family's tastes.

slow-cooked oriental chicken

Ruth Seitz, Columbus Junction, Iowa

Extremely tender chicken is smothered in a flavorful dark gravy in this easy and special entree. It's so nice to find another tantalizing way to serve chicken. Sprinkled with almonds, this is a dish I proudly serve to family or guests.

COOK TIME: 5 TO 6 HOURS

1 broiler/fryer chicken (3½ to 4 pounds), cut up

2 tablespoons vegetable oil

⅓ cup soy sauce

2 tablespoons brown sugar

2 tablespoons water

1 garlic clove, minced

1 teaspoon ground ginger

¼ cup slivered almonds

1 In a large skillet over medium heat, brown the chicken in oil on both sides. Transfer to a slow cooker. Combine the soy sauce, brown sugar, water, garlic and ginger; pour over chicken.

2 Cover and cook on high for 1 hour. Reduce heat to low; cook 4-5 hours longer or until the meat juices run clear. Remove chicken to a serving platter; sprinkle with almonds. Spoon juices over chicken or thicken if desired.

YIELD: 4-6 SERVINGS.

better safe than sorry

If you're not home during the entire slow-cooking process and there was a power outage, for food-safety reasons, it's best to throw away the food in your slow cooker even if it looks done.

cranberry chicken

COOK TIME: 6 TO 8 HOURS

- 1 cup fresh *or* frozen cranberries
- ¾ cup chopped onion
- ½ teaspoon salt
- ¼ teaspoon ground cinnamon
- ¼ teaspoon ground ginger
- 1 broiler/fryer chicken (about 3½ pounds), quartered and skin removed
- 1 cup orange juice
- 1 teaspoon grated orange peel
- 3 tablespoons butter, melted
- 3 tablespoons all-purpose flour
- 2 to 3 tablespoons brown sugar

Hot cooked noodles

1 In a slow cooker, combine first five ingredients; top with chicken. Pour orange juice over chicken and sprinkle with orange peel. Cover and cook on low for 5-6 hours or until meat juices run clear. Remove chicken; debone and cut up meat. Set aside and keep warm.

2 Combine the butter and flour until smooth; add to slow cooker. Cook on high until thickened, about 20 minutes. Stir in chicken and brown sugar; heat through. Serve over noodles.

YIELD: 4-6 SERVINGS.

Sandy Brooks, Tacoma, Washington

Cooking with cranberries is a happy habit for me. I like to include them because the fruit is filled with vitamin C—and my husband and son love the flavor. This chicken recipe is the one they request the most.

slow cooker chicken dinner

COOK TIME: 8½ HOURS

- 6 medium red potatoes, cut into chunks
- 4 medium carrots, cut into ½-inch pieces
- 4 boneless skinless chicken breast halves
- 1 can (10¾ ounces) condensed cream of chicken soup, undiluted
- 1 can (10¾ ounces) condensed cream of mushroom soup, undiluted
- ⅛ teaspoon garlic salt
- 2 to 4 tablespoons mashed potato flakes, optional

Place potatoes and carrots in a slow cooker. Top with chicken. Combine the soups and garlic salt; pour over chicken. Cover and cook on low for 8 hours. To thicken if desired, stir potato flakes into the gravy and cook 30 minutes longer.

YIELD: 4 SERVINGS.

Jenet Cattar, Neptune Beach, Florida

This meal-in-one, which includes juicy chicken and tasty veggies in a creamy sauce, is ready to eat when I get home from the office. It's great to walk in the door and smell this cooking.

chicken with stuffing

COOK TIME: 4 HOURS

- 4 boneless skinless chicken breast halves
- 1 can (10¾ ounces) condensed cream of chicken soup, undiluted
- 1¼ cups water
- ¼ cup butter, melted
- 1 package (6 ounces) corn bread stuffing mix

Place chicken in a greased slow cooker. Top with soup. In a bowl, combine the water, butter and stuffing mix; spoon over the chicken. Cover and cook on low for 4 hours or until chicken juices run clear.

YIELD: 4 SERVINGS.

Susan Kutz, Valley, Illinois

I need only five ingredients to create this comforting chicken topped with corn bread stuffing.

mandarin chicken

Aney Chatterton, Soda Springs, Idaho

Oranges and olives are elegantly paired in this different but delicious dish. The chicken is marinated, then cooked slowly in a flavorful sauce, so it stays moist.

COOK TIME: 7½ TO 8½ HOURS

- 1 broiler/fryer chicken (3 to 3½ pounds), cut up and skin removed
- 2 cups water
- 1 cup ketchup
- ¼ cup packed brown sugar
- ¼ cup soy sauce
- ¼ cup orange juice concentrate
- 2 teaspoons ground mustard
- 2 teaspoons salt
- 1 teaspoon pepper
- 1 teaspoon ground ginger
- 1 teaspoon garlic salt
- 3 tablespoons cornstarch
- ½ cup cold water
- 1 can (11 ounces) mandarin oranges, drained
- ½ cup whole pitted ripe olives
- 2 tablespoons chopped green pepper

Hot cooked rice

1 Place chicken in a large resealable plastic bag or glass dish. In a bowl, combine water, ketchup, brown sugar, soy sauce, orange juice concentrate, mustard, salt, pepper, ginger and garlic salt. Pour half over the chicken. Cover chicken and remaining marinade; refrigerate for 8 hours or overnight. Drain chicken, discarding marinade.

2 Place chicken in a slow cooker; add reserved marinade. Cover and cook on low for 7-8 hours. Combine cornstarch and cold water until smooth; stir into the chicken mixture. Add oranges, olives and green pepper. Cover and cook on high for 30-45 minutes or until thickened. Serve over rice.

YIELD: 4-6 SERVINGS.

turkey with cranberry sauce

COOK TIME: 4 TO 6 HOURS

- 2 boneless skinless turkey breast halves (about 4 pounds *each*)
- 1 can (14 ounces) jellied cranberry sauce
- ½ cup plus 2 tablespoons water, *divided*
- 1 envelope onion soup mix
- 2 tablespoons cornstarch

1 Cut each turkey breast in half; place in a 5-qt. slow cooker. In a bowl, combine the cranberry sauce, ½ cup water and soup mix; mix well. Pour over the turkey. Cover and cook on low for 4-6 hours or until the turkey is no longer pink and a meat thermometer reads 170°. Remove turkey and keep warm. Transfer the cranberry mixture to a small saucepan.

2 In a bowl, combine the cornstarch and remaining water until smooth. Bring cranberry mixture to a boil; stir in cornstarch mixture. Cook and stir for 2 minutes or until thickened. Slice turkey; serve with cranberry sauce.

YIELD: 20-25 SERVINGS.

Marie Ramsden, Fairgrove, Michigan

This is a very tasty and easy way to cook turkey in the slow cooker.

The sweet cranberry sauce complements the turkey nicely.

---

creamy chicken fettuccine

COOK TIME: 3 TO 4 HOURS

1½ **pounds boneless skinless chicken breasts, cut into cubes**

½ **teaspoon garlic powder**

½ **teaspoon onion powder**

⅛ **teaspoon pepper**

1 **can (10¾ ounces) condensed cream of chicken soup, undiluted**

1 **can (10¾ ounces) condensed cream of celery soup, undiluted**

4 **ounces process cheese (Velveeta), cubed**

1 **can (2¼ ounces) sliced ripe olives, drained**

1 **jar (2 ounces) diced pimientos, drained, optional**

1 **package (16 ounces) spinach fettuccine** *or* **spaghetti**

Thin breadsticks, optional

Melissa Cowser, Greenville, Texas

Convenient canned soup and process cheese hurry along the assembly of this creamy sauce loaded with delicious chunks of chicken.

1 Place the chicken in a slow cooker; sprinkle with garlic powder, onion powder and pepper. Top with soups. Cover and cook on high for 3-4 hours or until chicken juices run clear. Stir in the cheese, olives and pimientos if desired. Cover and cook until the cheese is melted.

2 Meanwhile, cook fettuccine according to package directions; drain. Serve with the chicken and breadsticks if desired.

YIELD: 6 SERVINGS.

herbed chicken and shrimp

Diana Knight, Reno, Nevada

Tender chicken and shrimp make a flavorful combination that's easy to prepare, yet elegant enough to serve at a dinner party. While I clean the house, it practically cooks itself. I serve it over hot cooked rice with crusty bread and a green salad.

COOK TIME: 4½ TO 5½ HOURS

- 1 teaspoon salt
- 1 teaspoon pepper
- 1 broiler/fryer chicken (3 to 4 pounds), cut up and skin removed
- ¼ cup butter
- 1 large onion, chopped
- 1 can (8 ounces) tomato sauce
- ½ cup white wine *or* chicken broth
- 1 garlic clove, minced
- 1 teaspoon dried basil
- 1 pound uncooked medium shrimp, peeled and deveined

1 Combine salt and pepper; rub over the chicken pieces. In a skillet, brown chicken on all sides in butter. Transfer to an ungreased slow cooker. In a bowl, combine the onion, tomato sauce, wine or broth, garlic and basil; pour over chicken.

2 Cover and cook on low for 4-5 hours or until chicken juices run clear. Add the shrimp and mix well. Cover and cook on high for 20-30 minutes or until shrimp turn pink.

YIELD: 4 SERVINGS.

slow-cooked orange chicken

COOK TIME: 4½ HOURS

- 1 broiler/fryer chicken (3 pounds), cut up and skin removed
- 3 cups orange juice
- 1 cup chopped celery
- 1 cup chopped green pepper
- 1 can (4 ounces) mushroom stems and pieces, drained
- 4 teaspoons dried minced onion
- 1 teaspoon dried parsley flakes
- ½ teaspoon salt
- ¼ teaspoon pepper
- 3 tablespoons cornstarch
- 3 tablespoons cold water

Hot cooked rice, optional

Combine the first nine ingredients in a slow cooker. Cover and cook on low for 4 hours or until meat juices run clear. Combine cornstarch and water until smooth; stir into cooking juices. Cover and cook on high for 30-45 minutes or until thickened. Serve over rice if desired.

YIELD: 4 SERVINGS.

Nancy Wit, Fremont, Nebraska

Everyone who tries this saucy chicken likes the taste, including my grandchildren. A hint of orange gives the chicken a delicious flavor. It travels well, and I often take it to potluck suppers.

turkey in a pot

COOK TIME: 5 TO 6 HOURS

1 boneless turkey breast (3 to 4 pounds), halved

1 can (16 ounces) whole-berry cranberry sauce

½ cup sugar

½ cup apple juice

1 tablespoon cider vinegar

2 garlic cloves, minced

1 teaspoon ground mustard

½ teaspoon ground cinnamon

¼ teaspoon ground cloves

¼ teaspoon ground allspice

2 tablespoons all-purpose flour

¼ cup cold water

¼ teaspoon browning sauce, optional

1 Place the turkey skin side up in a 5-qt. slow cooker. Combine cranberry sauce, sugar, apple juice, vinegar, garlic, mustard, cinnamon, cloves and allspice; pour over turkey. Cover and cook on low for 5-6 hours or until a meat thermometer reads 170°.

2 Remove turkey to a cutting board; keep warm. Strain cooking juices. In a saucepan, combine flour and water until smooth; gradually stir in strained juices. Bring to a boil; cook and stir for 2 minutes or until thickened. Stir in browning sauce if desired. Serve with sliced turkey.

YIELD: 12-16 SERVINGS.

Lois Woodward, Okeechobee, Florida

I use this recipe often for an easy Sunday dinner. The turkey breast gets a "holiday treatment" when served with cranberry gravy seasoned with cinnamon, cloves and allspice.

turkey enchiladas

Stella Schams, Tempe, Arizona

I was pleased to discover a different way to serve an economical cut of meat. I simmer turkey thighs with tomato sauce, green chilies and seasonings until they're tender and flavorful. Then I shred the turkey and serve it in tortillas with other fresh fixings.

COOK TIME: 6 TO 8 HOURS

- 2 turkey thighs *or* drumsticks (about 2 pounds)
- 1 can (8 ounces) tomato sauce
- 1 can (4 ounces) chopped green chilies
- 1/3 cup chopped onion
- 2 tablespoons Worcestershire sauce
- 1 to 2 tablespoons chili powder
- 1/4 teaspoon garlic powder
- 8 flour tortillas (7 inches)

Chopped green onions, sliced ripe olives, chopped tomatoes, shredded cheddar cheese, sour cream *and/or* shredded lettuce

1 Remove skin from the turkey. Place in a 5-qt. slow cooker. Combine the tomato sauce, chilies, onion, Worcestershire sauce, chili powder and garlic powder; pour over turkey. Cover; cook on low for 6-8 hours or until the turkey is tender.

2 Remove the turkey; shred the meat with a fork and return to the slow cooker. Heat through. Spoon about 1/2 cup of the turkey mixture down the center of each tortilla. Add the toppings of your choice. Fold bottom of the tortilla over the filling and roll up.

YIELD: 4 SERVINGS.

southwestern chicken

COOK TIME: 3 TO 4 HOURS

2 cans (15¼ ounces *each*) whole kernel corn, drained

1 can (15 ounces) black beans, rinsed and drained

1 jar (16 ounces) chunky salsa, *divided*

6 boneless skinless chicken breast halves

1 cup (4 ounces) shredded cheddar cheese

Combine the corn, black beans and ½ cup of salsa in a slow cooker. Top with chicken; pour the remaining salsa over chicken. Cover and cook on high for 3-4 hours or on low for 7-8 hours or until meat juices run clear. Sprinkle with cheese; cover and cook until cheese is melted, about 5 minutes.

YIELD: 6 SERVINGS.

Karen Waters, Laurel, Maryland

Prepared salsa and convenient canned corn and beans add fun color, texture and flavor to this tender chicken dish. I serve it with rice and a salad. Our children love it.

king-size drumsticks

8 TO 10 HOURS

1 **can (10 ounces) enchilada sauce**

1 **can (4 ounces) chopped green chilies, drained**

1 **teaspoon dried oregano**

½ **teaspoon garlic salt**

½ **teaspoon ground cumin**

6 **turkey drumsticks**

3 **tablespoons cornstarch**

3 **tablespoons cold water**

1 In a bowl, combine first five ingredients. Place the drumsticks in a 5-qt. slow cooker; top with sauce. Cover; cook on low for 8-10 hours or until a meat thermometer reads 180°.

2 Remove turkey and keep warm. Strain sauce into a saucepan. Combine cornstarch and water until smooth; stir into the pan. Bring to a boil; cook and stir for 2 minutes or until thickened. Serve with turkey.

YIELD: 6 SERVINGS.

Taste of Home Test Kitchen, Greendale, Wisconsin

Let your slow cooker do the work for you when you serve these savory turkey legs. In this recipe, enchilada sauce, green chilies and cumin give this main dish a zesty royal treatment.

stuffed chicken rolls

Jean Sherwood, Kenneth City, Florida

The wonderful aroma of this moist delicious chicken cooking sparks our appetites. The ham and cheese rolled inside is a tasty surprise. When I prepared this impressive main dish for a church luncheon, I received lots of compliments. The rolls are especially nice served over rice or pasta.

COOK TIME: 4 TO 5 HOURS

- 6 boneless skinless chicken breast halves
- 6 slices fully cooked ham
- 6 slices Swiss cheese
- 1/4 cup all-purpose flour
- 1/4 cup grated Parmesan cheese
- 1/2 teaspoon rubbed sage
- 1/4 teaspoon paprika
- 1/4 teaspoon pepper
- 1/4 cup vegetable oil
- 1 can (10 3/4 ounces) condensed cream of chicken soup, undiluted
- 1/2 cup chicken broth

Chopped fresh parsley, optional

1 Flatten chicken to 1/8-in. thickness. Place 1 slice ham and cheese on each breast. Roll up and tuck in ends; secure with a toothpick. Combine the flour, Parmesan cheese, sage, paprika and pepper; coat chicken on all sides. Cover and refrigerate for 1 hour.

2 In a large skillet, brown chicken in oil over medium-high heat. Transfer to a 5-qt. slow cooker. Combine soup and broth; pour over chicken. Cover and cook on low for 4-5 hours. Remove toothpicks. Garnish with parsley if desired.

YIELD: 6 SERVINGS.

turkey with mushroom sauce

COOK TIME: 7 TO 8 HOURS

- 1 boneless turkey breast (3 pounds), halved
- 2 tablespoons butter, melted
- 2 tablespoons dried parsley flakes
- 1/2 teaspoon dried tarragon
- 1/2 teaspoon salt
- 1/8 teaspoon pepper
- 1 jar (4 1/2 ounces) sliced mushrooms, drained *or* 1 cup sliced fresh mushrooms
- 1/2 cup white wine *or* chicken broth
- 2 tablespoons cornstarch
- 1/4 cup cold water

1 Place the turkey, skin side up, in a slow cooker. Brush with butter. Sprinkle with parsley, tarragon, salt and pepper. Top with mushrooms. Pour wine or broth over all. Cover and cook on low for 7-8 hours. Remove turkey and keep warm. Skim fat from cooking juices.

2 In a saucepan, combine the cornstarch and water until smooth. Gradually add the cooking juices. Bring to a boil; cook and stir for 2 minutes or until thickened. Serve with the turkey.

YIELD: 12 SERVINGS (2 1/2 CUPS SAUCE).

Myra Innes, Auburn, Kansas

When we were first married, I didn't have an oven, so I made this tender turkey in the slow cooker. Now I rely on this recipe because it frees up the oven to make other dishes.

red pepper chicken

COOK TIME: 6 HOURS

4 boneless skinless chicken breast halves

1 can (15 ounces) black beans, rinsed and drained

1 jar (15 ounces) roasted red peppers, undrained

1 can (14½ ounces) Mexican stewed tomatoes, undrained

1 large onion, chopped

½ teaspoon salt

Pepper to taste

Hot cooked rice

1 Place the chicken in a slow cooker. In a bowl, combine the beans, red peppers, tomatoes, onion, salt and pepper. Pour over the chicken.

2 Cover and cook on low for 6 hours or until chicken juices run clear. Serve over rice.

YIELD: 4 SERVINGS.

Piper Spiwak, Vienna, Virginia

Chicken breasts are treated to a bevy of black beans, red peppers and tomatoes in this Southwestern supper. We love this colorful dish over rice cooked in chicken broth.

creamy italian chicken

Maura McGee, Tallahassee, Florida

This tender chicken in a creamy sauce gets fast flavor from a salad dressing mix. Served over rice or pasta, it's rich, delicious and special enough for company.

COOK TIME: 4 HOURS

- 4 boneless skinless chicken breast halves
- 1 envelope Italian salad dressing mix
- ¼ cup water
- 1 package (8 ounces) cream cheese, softened
- 1 can (10¾ ounces) condensed cream of chicken soup, undiluted
- 1 can (4 ounces) mushroom stems and pieces, drained

Hot cooked rice *or* noodles

Place the chicken in a slow cooker. Combine salad dressing mix and water; pour over chicken. Cover and cook on low for 3 hours. In a small mixing bowl, beat cream cheese and soup until blended. Stir in mushrooms. Pour over chicken. Cook 1 hour longer or until chicken juices run clear. Serve over rice or noodles.

YIELD: 4 SERVINGS.

chicken with vegetables

COOK TIME: 5 HOURS

- 1 cup sliced fresh mushrooms
- 4 chicken legs, skin removed
- 4 chicken thighs, skin removed
- 4 celery ribs, sliced
- 1 cup sliced zucchini
- 1 cup sliced carrots
- 1 medium onion, sliced
- 1 cup tomato juice
- 1/2 cup chicken broth
- 1 garlic clove, minced
- 1/4 teaspoon paprika

Pepper to taste

- 3 tablespoons cornstarch
- 3 tablespoons cold water

Hot cooked rice

1 Place mushrooms and chicken in a slow cooker. Add the celery, zucchini, carrots, onion, tomato juice, broth, garlic, paprika and pepper. Cover and cook on low for 5 hours or until meat juices run clear.

2 Remove chicken and vegetables and keep warm. Transfer cooking juices to a saucepan; skim fat. Combine the cornstarch and water until smooth; add to the juices. Bring to a boil; cook and stir for 2 minutes or until thickened. Pour over chicken and vegetables; serve over rice.

YIELD: 4 SERVINGS.

Norlene Razak, Tye, Texas

You'll be surprised at how easily this tender chicken entree comes together.
It's simple, delicious and a great way to get your family to eat vegetables.

turkey in cream sauce

COOK TIME: 7 TO 8 HOURS

1¼ cups white wine *or* chicken broth

1 medium onion, chopped

2 garlic cloves, minced

2 bay leaves

2 teaspoons dried rosemary, crushed

½ teaspoon pepper

3 turkey breast tenderloins
(¾ pound *each*)

3 tablespoons cornstarch

½ cup half-and-half cream *or* milk

½ teaspoon salt

1 In a slow cooker, combine wine or broth, onion, garlic and bay leaves. Combine rosemary and pepper; rub over turkey. Place in slow cooker. Cover; cook on low 7-8 hours or until meat is tender. Remove turkey; keep warm. Strain cooking juices; pour into a saucepan.

2 Combine cornstarch, cream and salt until smooth; gradually add to juices. Bring to a boil; cook and stir 2 minutes or until thickened. Slice turkey; serve with sauce.

YIELD: 9 SERVINGS.

Kathy-Jo Winterbottom, Pottstown, Pennsylvania

I've been relying on this recipe for tender turkey since I first moved out on my own years ago. I serve it whenever I invite new guests to the house, and I'm constantly sharing the recipe.

you've got good taste

Always taste the finished dish before serving to adjust seasonings to your preference, since long cooking times can dilute the strength of herbs and spices. Consider adding a dash of salt, pepper, lemon juice or minced fresh herbs.

creamy chicken and beef

COOK TIME: 8 TO 9 HOURS

- 6 bacon strips
- 1 package (2½ ounces) thinly sliced dried beef
- 6 boneless skinless chicken breast halves
- ¼ cup all-purpose flour
- 1 can (10¾ ounces) condensed cream of mushroom soup, undiluted
- ¼ cup sour cream

Hot cooked noodles

1 In a skillet, partially cook bacon over medium heat. Drain on paper towels. Place beef in a greased slow cooker. Fold chicken pieces in half and wrap a bacon strip around each; place over the beef. Combine the flour, soup and sour cream until blended; spread over chicken.

2 Cover and cook on low for 8-9 hours or until chicken juices run clear. Serve over noodles.

YIELD: 6 SERVINGS.

Jane Thocher, Hart, Michigan

I relied on this tender chicken dish often when our children lived at home. Since it cooked while I was at work, the only thing left to do was prepare noodles and a salad.

chicken in mushroom sauce

COOK TIME: 4 TO 5 HOURS

- 4 boneless skinless chicken breast halves
- 1 can (10¾ ounces) condensed cream of mushroom soup, undiluted
- 1 cup (8 ounces) sour cream
- 4 bacon strips, cooked and crumbled

Place chicken in a slow cooker. Combine soup and sour cream; pour over chicken. Cover and cook on low for 4-5 hours or until chicken juices run clear. Sprinkle with bacon.

YIELD: 4 SERVINGS.

Kathy Gallagher, La Crosse, Wisconsin

Bacon and sour cream add richness to a simple sauce that really dresses up everyday chicken.

pork, lamb & seafood

206

210

Expand your appreciation of the slow cooker by trying these new recipes using standby ingredients and a selection of pork, lamb or seafood. Every one has been kitchen-tested for delicious results.

Just five ingredients is all it takes to turn out Tender Pork Roast (p. 206) and impress guests. But why save the special dishes for company? Surprise your family with sensational Slow-Cooked Ham 'n' Broccoli (p. 210) any night of the week.

sesame pork ribs

COOK TIME: 5 TO 6 HOURS

- ¾ cup packed brown sugar
- ½ cup soy sauce
- ½ cup ketchup
- ¼ cup honey
- 2 tablespoons white wine vinegar
- 3 garlic cloves, minced
- 1 teaspoon ground ginger
- 1 teaspoon salt
- ¼ to ½ teaspoon crushed red pepper flakes
- 5 pounds country-style pork ribs
- 1 medium onion, sliced
- 2 tablespoons sesame seeds, toasted
- 2 tablespoons chopped green onions

1 In a large bowl, combine the first nine ingredients. Add ribs and turn to coat. Place onion in a 5-qt. slow cooker; arrange ribs on top and pour sauce over.

2 Cover and cook on low for 5-6 hours or until a meat thermometer reads 160°-170°. Place ribs on a serving platter; sprinkle with sesame seeds and green onions.

YIELD: 6 SERVINGS.

Sandy Alexander, Fayetteville, North Carolina

No one ever believes how little effort it takes to make these tasty tempting ribs. The flavor of the lightly sweet and tangy sauce penetrates through the meat as the ribs simmer in the slow cooker.

sunday pot roast

COOK TIME: 8 HOURS

 1 teaspoon dried oregano

½ teaspoon onion salt

½ teaspoon pepper

½ teaspoon caraway seed

¼ teaspoon garlic salt

 1 boneless pork loin roast (3½ to 4 pounds), trimmed

 6 medium carrots, peeled and cut into 1½-inch pieces

 3 large potatoes, peeled and quartered

 3 small onions, quartered

1½ cups beef broth

⅓ cup all-purpose flour

⅓ cup cold water

¼ teaspoon browning sauce, optional

1 Combine the seasonings; rub over roast. Wrap in plastic wrap and refrigerate overnight. Place carrots, potatoes and onions in a slow cooker; add broth. Unwrap roast and place in the slow cooker. Cover and cook on high for 2 hours. Reduce heat to low and cook 6 hours longer or until a meat thermometer reads 160°.

2 Transfer the roast and vegetables to a serving platter; keep warm. Pour broth into a saucepan. Combine the flour and water until smooth; stir into broth. Bring to a boil; boil and whisk for 2 minutes. Add the browning sauce if desired. Serve with the roast.

YIELD: 12-14 SERVINGS.

Brandy Schaefer, Glen Carbon, Illinois

This recipe proves you don't have to stand over a hot stove to prepare a delicious, down-home dinner like Grandma used to make. The roast turns out moist and tasty every time.

sweet 'n' sour ribs

Dorothy Voelz, Champaign, Illinois

If you're looking for a change from typical barbecue ribs, you'll enjoy this recipe my mom always prepared on birthdays and special occasions. The tender ribs have a slight sweet-and-sour taste that my family loves. I usually serve them with garlic mashed potatoes and a salad or coleslaw.

COOK TIME: 8 TO 10 HOURS

3 to 4 pounds boneless country-style pork ribs

1 can (20 ounces) pineapple tidbits, undrained

2 cans (8 ounces *each*) tomato sauce

½ cup thinly sliced onion

½ cup thinly sliced green pepper

½ cup packed brown sugar

¼ cup cider vinegar

¼ cup tomato paste

2 tablespoons Worcestershire sauce

1 garlic clove, minced

Salt and pepper to taste

1 Place the ribs in an ungreased slow cooker. In a bowl, combine the remaining ingredients; pour over the ribs.

2 Cover and cook on low for 8-10 hours or until the meat is tender. Thicken the sauce if desired.

YIELD: 8 SERVINGS.

polish kraut and apples

COOK TIME: 4 TO 5 HOURS

- 1 can (14 ounces) sauerkraut, rinsed and well drained
- 1 pound fully cooked Polish sausage *or* kielbasa, cut into 2-inch pieces
- 3 medium tart apples, peeled and cut into eighths
- ½ cup packed brown sugar
- ½ teaspoon caraway seed, optional
- ⅛ teaspoon pepper
- ¾ cup apple juice

Place half of the sauerkraut in an ungreased slow cooker. Top with sausage, apples, brown sugar, caraway seed if desired and pepper. Top with remaining sauerkraut. Pour the apple juice over all. Cover and cook on low for 4-5 hours or until apples are tender.

YIELD: 4 SERVINGS.

Caren Markee, Cary, Illinois

My family loves this hearty, comforting meal on cold winter nights. The tender apples, brown sugar and smoked sausage give this dish fantastic flavor. I like making it because the prep time is very short.

ham and hash browns

COOK TIME: 7 TO 8 HOURS

- 1 package (28 ounces) frozen O'Brien hash brown potatoes
- 2 cups cubed fully cooked ham
- 1 jar (2 ounces) diced pimientos, drained
- 1 can (10¾ ounces) condensed cheddar cheese soup, undiluted
- ¾ cup milk
- ¼ teaspoon pepper

In a slow cooker, combine the potatoes, ham and pimientos. In a bowl, combine soup, milk and pepper; pour over the potato mixture. Cover and cook on low for 7-8 hours or until potatoes are tender.

YIELD: 4 SERVINGS.

Marlene Muckenhirn, Delano, Minnesota

You just can't beat the slow cooker for convenience…I use mine two or three times a week all year-round. This is a new way to prepare an old-fashioned favorite.

---

orange pork roast

COOK TIME: 8 HOURS

- 1 pork shoulder roast (3 to 4 pounds), trimmed
- ½ teaspoon salt
- ⅛ teaspoon pepper
- 1 can (6 ounces) frozen orange juice concentrate, thawed
- ¼ cup honey
- ⅛ teaspoon ground cloves
- ⅛ teaspoon ground nutmeg
- 3 tablespoons all-purpose flour
- ¼ cup cold water

1 Sprinkle roast with salt and pepper; place in a slow cooker. Combine orange juice concentrate, honey, cloves and nutmeg; pour over pork. Cover and cook on high for 2 hours. Reduce heat to low and cook 6 hours longer. Remove meat to a serving platter; cover and keep warm.

2 Skim and discard fat from cooking liquid; pour into a saucepan. Combine flour and cold water until smooth; stir into cooking liquid. Bring to a boil; stir for 2 minutes. Serve with the roast.

YIELD: 8 SERVINGS.

Nancy Medeiros, Sparks, Nevada

Overcooking can cause pork roasts to be dry and tough. But slow cooking and this recipe's succulent orange sauce guarantee that the meat turns out moist and tender.

easy and elegant ham

Denise DiPace, Medford, New Jersey

I fix this moist tender ham to serve my large family. Covered with colorful pineapple slices, cherries and orange glaze, its show-stopping appearance and flavor appeal to both children and adults.

COOK TIME: 6 TO 7 HOURS

- 2 cans (20 ounces *each*) sliced pineapple
- 1 fully cooked boneless ham (about 6 pounds), halved
- 1 jar (6 ounces) maraschino cherries, well drained
- 1 jar (12 ounces) orange marmalade

1 Drain pineapple, reserving juice; set juice aside. Place half of the pineapple in an ungreased 5-qt. slow cooker. Top with the ham. Add cherries, remaining pineapple and reserved pineapple juice. Spoon marmalade over ham. Cover and cook on low for 6-7 hours or until heated through.

2 Remove to a warm serving platter. Let stand for 10-15 minutes before slicing. Serve the pineapple and cherries with the sliced ham.

YIELD: 18-20 SERVINGS.

avoiding a sticky situation

Slow cooker inserts are fairly easy to clean with hot soapy water. For even faster cleanup, coat the bottom and sides of the insert with nonstick cooking spray before putting in the food.

tangy pork chops

COOK TIME: 5½ TO 6½ HOURS

- 4 pork chops (½ inch thick)
- ½ teaspoon salt
- ⅛ teaspoon pepper
- 2 medium onions, chopped
- 2 celery ribs, chopped
- 1 large green pepper, sliced
- 1 can (14½ ounces) stewed tomatoes
- ½ cup ketchup
- 2 tablespoons cider vinegar
- 2 tablespoons brown sugar
- 2 tablespoons Worcestershire sauce
- 1 tablespoon lemon juice
- 1 beef bouillon cube
- 2 tablespoons cornstarch
- 2 tablespoons water

Hot cooked rice, optional

1 Place chops in a slow cooker; sprinkle with salt and pepper. Add the onions, celery, green pepper and tomatoes. Combine the ketchup, vinegar, sugar, Worcestershire sauce, lemon juice and bouillon; pour over vegetables. Cover and cook on low for 5-6 hours.

2 Mix the cornstarch and water until smooth; stir into liquid in slow cooker. Cover and cook on high for 30 minutes or until thickened. Serve over rice if desired.

YIELD: 4 SERVINGS.

Karol Hines, Kitty Hawk, North Carolina

Fancy enough for company, these mouth-watering pork chops also make a great family meal. I usually have all the ingredients on hand.

saucy scalloped potatoes

COOK TIME: 7 HOURS

 4 cups thinly sliced peeled potatoes (about 2 pounds)

 1 can (10¾ ounces) cream of celery *or* mushroom soup, undiluted

 1 can (12 ounces) evaporated milk

 1 large onion, sliced

 2 tablespoons butter

 ½ teaspoon salt

 ¼ teaspoon pepper

 1½ cups chopped fully cooked ham

1 In a slow cooker, combine the first seven ingredients; mix well. Cover and cook on high for 1 hour.

2 Stir in ham. Reduce heat to low; cook 6-8 hours longer or until potatoes are tender.

YIELD: 4-6 MAIN-DISH OR 8-12 SIDE-DISH SERVINGS.

Elaine Kane, Keizer, Oregon

For old-fashioned flavor, try these scalloped potatoes. They cook up tender, creamy and comforting. Chopped ham adds a hearty touch.

san francisco chops

COOK TIME: 7½ TO 8½ HOURS

4 bone-in pork loin chops (1 inch thick)

1 to 2 tablespoons vegetable oil

1 garlic clove, minced

¼ cup soy sauce

¼ cup red wine *or* chicken broth

2 tablespoons brown sugar

¼ teaspoon crushed red pepper flakes

1 tablespoon cornstarch

1 tablespoon cold water

Hot cooked rice

1 In a skillet, brown pork chops in oil; transfer to a slow cooker. Add garlic to drippings; cook and stir for about 1 minute or until golden. Stir in next four ingredients; cook and stir until sugar is dissolved. Pour over chops. Cover and cook on low for 7-8 hours or until meat is tender.

2 Remove chops. Combine cornstarch and cold water until smooth; gradually stir into slow cooker. Return chops to slow cooker. Cover and cook for at least 30 minutes or until slightly thickened. Serve over rice.

YIELD: 4 SERVINGS.

Tara Bonesteel, Dayton, New Jersey

It's easy to please friends and family with these fast-to-fix chops. Simmered in a tangy sauce all day, they're so moist and delicious by dinnertime they practically melt in your mouth.

chalupa

COOK TIME: 8 HOURS

1 cup dried pinto beans

3½ cups water

¼ cup chopped onion

1 can (4 ounces) chopped green chilies

1 garlic clove, minced

1 tablespoon chili powder

1½ teaspoons salt

1½ teaspoons ground cumin

½ teaspoon dried oregano

1 boneless pork shoulder roast (1½ pounds), trimmed

1 package (10½ ounces) corn chips

¼ cup sliced green onions

Shredded lettuce

Shredded cheddar cheese

Chopped fresh tomatoes

Salsa

1 Place beans and enough water to cover in a 3-qt. saucepan. Bring to a boil; boil for 2 minutes. Remove from the heat; let stand for 1 hour. Drain beans and discard liquid. In a slow cooker, combine water, onion, chilies, garlic, chili powder, salt, cumin and oregano. Add roast and beans. Cover and cook on high for 2 hours. Reduce heat to low and cook 6 hours longer or until pork is very tender.

2 Remove roast and shred with a fork. Drain beans, reserving cooking liquid in a saucepan. Combine beans and meat; set aside. Skim and discard fat from cooking liquid; bring to a boil. Boil, uncovered, for 20 minutes or until reduced to 1½ cups. Add meat and bean mixture; heat through. Spoon meat mixture over corn chips; top with green onions, lettuce, cheese, tomatoes and salsa.

YIELD: 6-8 SERVINGS.

Ginny Becker, Torrington, Wyoming

This is such a refreshing change of pace from traditional chili. It's also fun to serve to guests. Nearly everyone who's sampled it has requested the recipe.

tender 'n' tangy ribs

Denise Hathaway Valasek, Perrysburg, Ohio

These ribs are so simple to prepare. Serve them at noon…or let them cook all day for falling-off-the-bone tenderness.

COOK TIME: 4 TO 6 HOURS

- ¾ to 1 cup vinegar
- ½ cup ketchup
- 2 tablespoons sugar
- 2 tablespoons Worcestershire sauce
- 1 garlic clove, minced
- 1 teaspoon ground mustard
- 1 teaspoon paprika
- ½ to 1 teaspoon salt
- ⅛ teaspoon pepper
- 2 pounds pork spareribs
- 1 tablespoon vegetable oil

Combine the first nine ingredients in a slow cooker. Cut the ribs into serving-size pieces; brown in a skillet in oil. Transfer to slow cooker. Cover and cook on low for 4-6 hours or until tender.

YIELD: 2-3 SERVINGS.

ham with cherry sauce

COOK TIME: 4 TO 5 HOURS

- 1 boneless fully cooked ham (3 to 4 pounds)
- 1/2 cup apple jelly
- 2 teaspoons prepared mustard
- 2/3 cup ginger ale, *divided*
- 1 can (21 ounces) cherry pie filling
- 2 tablespoons cornstarch

1 Score surface of ham, making diamond shapes 1/2 in. deep. In a small bowl, combine jelly, mustard and 1 tablespoon ginger ale; rub over scored surface of ham. Cut ham in half; place in a 5-qt. slow cooker. Cover and cook on low for 4-5 hours or until a meat thermometer reads 140° and the ham is heated through. Baste with cooking juices toward end of cooking.

2 For sauce, place pie filling in a saucepan. Combine cornstarch and remaining ginger ale; stir into pie filling until blended. Bring to a boil; cook and stir for 2 minutes or until thickened. Serve over ham.

YIELD: 12-16 SERVINGS.

Carol Lee Jones, Taylors, South Carolina

I'm always happy to fix this delicious ham topped with a thick cherry sauce. It's such a favorite that I've served it at Easter dinners, church breakfasts and a friend's wedding brunch.

ham with cherry sauce

COOK TIME: 4 TO 5 HOURS

1 boneless fully cooked ham
   (3 to 4 pounds)

$\frac{1}{2}$ cup apple jelly

2 teaspoons prepared mustard

$\frac{2}{3}$ cup ginger ale, *divided*

1 can (21 ounces) cherry pie filling

2 tablespoons cornstarch

1 Score surface of ham, making diamond shapes $\frac{1}{2}$ in. deep. In a small bowl, combine jelly, mustard and 1 tablespoon ginger ale; rub over scored surface of ham. Cut ham in half; place in a 5-qt. slow cooker. Cover and cook on low for 4-5 hours or until a meat thermometer reads 140° and the ham is heated through. Baste with cooking juices toward end of cooking.

2 For sauce, place pie filling in a saucepan. Combine cornstarch and remaining ginger ale; stir into pie filling until blended. Bring to a boil; cook and stir for 2 minutes or until thickened. Serve over ham.

YIELD: 12-16 SERVINGS.

Carol Lee Jones, Taylors, South Carolina

I'm always happy to fix this delicious ham topped with a thick cherry sauce. It's such a favorite that I've served it at Easter dinners, church breakfasts and a friend's wedding brunch.

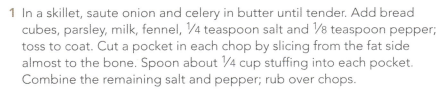

herb-stuffed chops

COOK TIME: 8 TO 9 HOURS

- ¾ cup chopped onion
- ¼ cup chopped celery
- 2 tablespoons butter
- 2 cups day-old bread cubes
- ½ cup minced fresh parsley
- ⅓ cup evaporated milk
- 1 teaspoon fennel seed, crushed
- 1½ teaspoons salt, *divided*
- ½ teaspoon pepper, *divided*
- 6 rib *or* loin pork chops (1 inch thick)
- 1 tablespoon vegetable oil
- ¾ cup white wine *or* chicken broth

1 In a skillet, saute onion and celery in butter until tender. Add bread cubes, parsley, milk, fennel, ¼ teaspoon salt and ⅛ teaspoon pepper; toss to coat. Cut a pocket in each chop by slicing from the fat side almost to the bone. Spoon about ¼ cup stuffing into each pocket. Combine the remaining salt and pepper; rub over chops.

2 In a skillet, brown the chops in oil; transfer to a slow cooker. Pour wine or broth over the chops. Cover and cook on low for 8-9 hours or until meat juices run clear.

YIELD: 6 SERVINGS.

Diane Seeger, New Springfield, Ohio

Guests will think you stayed home all day when you serve these tender stuffed chops. I often share this recipe with new brides because I know it will become one of their favorites.

tender pork roast

LuVerne Peterson, Minneapolis, Minnesota

This easy, melt-in-your-mouth pork roast is wonderful to serve to company because it never fails to please.

COOK TIME: 8 TO 9 HOURS

- 1 boneless pork roast (about 3 pounds)
- 1 can (8 ounces) tomato sauce
- ¾ cup soy sauce
- ½ cup sugar
- 2 teaspoons ground mustard

Cut roast in half; place in a 5-qt. slow cooker. Combine remaining ingredients; pour over roast. Cover and cook on low for 8-9 hours or until a meat thermometer reads 160°-170°. Remove roast to a serving platter and keep warm. If desired, skim fat from pan juices and thicken for gravy.

YIELD: 8 SERVINGS.

chicken fried chops

COOK TIME: 6 TO 8 HOURS

- ½ cup all-purpose flour
- 2 teaspoons salt
- 1½ teaspoons ground mustard
- ½ teaspoon garlic powder
- 6 pork loin chops (¾ inch thick), trimmed
- 2 tablespoons vegetable oil
- 1 can (10¾ ounces) condensed cream of chicken soup, undiluted
- ⅓ cup water

1 In a shallow bowl, combine flour, salt, mustard and garlic powder; dredge pork chops. In a skillet, brown the chops on both sides in oil. Place in a slow cooker. Combine soup and water; pour over the chops.

2 Cover and cook on low for 6-8 hours or until meat is tender. If desired, thicken pan juices and serve with the pork chops.

YIELD: 6 SERVINGS.

Connie Slocum, Brunswick, Georgia

It takes only a few minutes to brown the meat before assembling this savory meal. The pork chops simmer all day in a flavorful sauce until they're fork-tender.

sausage sauerkraut supper

COOK TIME: 8 TO 9 HOURS

- 4 cups carrot chunks (2-inch pieces)
- 4 cups red potato chunks
- 2 cans (14 ounces *each*) sauerkraut, rinsed and drained
- 2½ pounds fresh Polish sausage, cut into 3-inch pieces
- 1 medium onion, thinly sliced
- 3 garlic cloves, minced
- 1½ cups dry white wine *or* chicken broth
- 1 teaspoon pepper
- ½ teaspoon caraway seed

1 In a 5-qt. slow cooker, layer carrots, potatoes and sauerkraut. In a skillet, brown the sausage; transfer to the slow cooker (slow cooker will be full). Reserve 1 tablespoon drippings in skillet; saute onion and garlic until tender. Gradually add wine or broth. Bring to a boil; stir to loosen browned bits. Stir in pepper and caraway. Pour over sausage.

2 Cover and cook on low for 8-9 hours or until the vegetables are tender and the sausage is no longer pink.

YIELD: 10-12 SERVINGS.

Joalyce Graham, St. Petersburg, Florida

With big tender chunks of sausage, potatoes and carrots, this meal-in-one has old-world flavor that will satisfy the heartiest of appetites. A co-worker often made a big pot of this for our office staff, and it always disappeared in a hurry.

pork and cabbage dinner

COOK TIME: 8 HOURS

- 1 pound carrots
- 1½ cups water
- 1 envelope onion soup mix
- 2 garlic cloves, minced
- ½ teaspoon celery seed
- 1 boneless pork shoulder roast (4 to 6 pounds)
- ½ teaspoon salt
- ¼ teaspoon pepper
- 1½ pounds cabbage, cut into 2-inch pieces

1 Cut carrots in half lengthwise, then into 2-in. pieces. Place in a 5-qt. slow cooker. Add water, soup mix, garlic and celery seed. Cut roast in half; place over carrot mixture. Sprinkle with salt and pepper. Cover; cook on high for 2 hours.

2 Reduce heat to low; cook for 4 hours. Add cabbage; cook 2 hours longer or until the cabbage is tender and a meat thermometer reads 160°. Remove meat and vegetables to a serving plate; keep warm. If desired, thicken pan drippings for gravy and serve with the roast.

YIELD: 8-10 SERVINGS.

Trina Hinkel, Minneapolis, Minnesota

I put on this pork roast in the morning to avoid that evening dinner rush.
All I do is fix potatoes, and our family can sit down to a filling supper.

hot dogs 'n' beans

COOK TIME: 7 TO 8 HOURS

- 3 cans (two 28 ounces, one 16 ounces) pork and beans
- 1 package (1 pound) hot dogs, halved lengthwise and cut into 1-inch pieces
- 1 large onion, chopped
- ½ cup packed brown sugar
- 3 tablespoons prepared mustard
- 4 bacon strips, cooked and crumbled

In a slow cooker, combine all ingredients; mix well. Cover and cook on low for 7-8 hours.

YIELD: 10 SERVINGS.

June Formanek, Belle Plaine, Iowa

You'll please kids of all ages with this tasty combination that's good for casual get-togethers. I frequently fix this when the whole family is home.

slow-cooked ham 'n' broccoli

Jill Pennington, Jacksonville, Florida

This sensational dish is so wonderful to come home to, especially on a cool fall or winter day. It's a delicious way to use up leftover holiday ham, too.

COOK TIME: 2 TO 3 HOURS

- 3 cups cubed fully cooked ham
- 1 package (10 ounces) frozen chopped broccoli, thawed
- 1 can (10¾ ounces) condensed cream of mushroom soup, undiluted
- 1 jar (8 ounces) process cheese sauce
- 1 can (8 ounces) sliced water chestnuts, drained
- 1¼ cups uncooked instant rice
- 1 cup milk
- 1 celery rib, chopped
- 1 medium onion, chopped
- ⅛ to ¼ teaspoon pepper
- ½ teaspoon paprika

In a slow cooker, combine the first 10 ingredients; mix well. Cover and cook on high for 2-3 hours or until the rice is tender. Let stand for 10 minutes before serving. Sprinkle with paprika.

YIELD: 6-8 SERVINGS.

teriyaki pork roast

COOK TIME: 7 TO 8 HOURS

¾ cup unsweetened apple juice

2 tablespoons sugar

2 tablespoons soy sauce

1 tablespoon vinegar

1 teaspoon ground ginger

¼ teaspoon garlic powder

⅛ teaspoon pepper

1 boneless pork loin roast (about 3 pounds), halved

7½ teaspoons cornstarch

3 tablespoons cold water

1 Combine the first seven ingredients in a greased slow cooker. Add roast and turn to coat. Cover and cook on low for 7-8 hours or until a thermometer inserted into the roast reads 160°. Remove roast and keep warm.

2 In a saucepan, combine cornstarch and cold water until smooth; stir in cooking juices. Bring to a boil; cook and stir for 2 minutes or until thickened. Serve with the roast.

YIELD: 8 SERVINGS.

Roxanne Hulsey, Gainesville, Georgia

Since my husband works full time and attends school, I do a great deal around the house. I'm always looking for no-fuss recipes, so I was thrilled to find this one.

pork carnitas

COOK TIME: 9 TO 11 HOURS

- 1 boneless pork shoulder *or* loin roast (2 to 3 pounds), trimmed and cut into 3-inch cubes
- ½ cup lime juice
- 1 teaspoon salt
- ½ teaspoon pepper
- ½ teaspoon crushed red pepper flakes
- 12 flour tortillas (7 inches), warmed
- 2 cups (8 ounces) shredded cheddar *or* Monterey Jack cheese
- 2 medium avocados, peeled and diced
- 2 medium tomatoes, diced
- 1 medium onion, diced

Shredded lettuce

Minced fresh cilantro, optional

Salsa

1 In a slow cooker, combine the pork, lime juice, salt, pepper and pepper flakes. Cover and cook on high for 1 hour; stir. Reduce heat to low and cook 8-10 hours longer or until the meat is very tender.

2 Shred the pork with a fork (it may look somewhat pink). Spoon about ⅓ cup of filling down the center of each tortilla. Top with cheese, avocados, tomatoes, onion, lettuce and cilantro if desired. Fold in bottom and sides of tortilla. Serve with salsa.

YIELD: 12 SERVINGS.

Tracy Byers, Corvallis, Oregon

I use this recipe often when entertaining. I set out all the toppings, and folks have fun assembling their own carnitas. Because I can prepare everything in advance, I get to spend more time with my guests.

---

slow-cooked lamb chops

Sandra McKenzie, Braham, Minnesota

Chops are without a doubt the cut of lamb we like best. The aroma is irresistible, and they come out of the slow cooker so tender.

COOK TIME: 4 TO 6 HOURS

- 1 medium onion, sliced
- 1 teaspoon dried oregano
- 1/2 teaspoon dried thyme
- 1/2 teaspoon garlic powder
- 1/4 teaspoon salt
- 1/8 teaspoon pepper
- 8 loin lamb chops (about 1 3/4 pounds)
- 2 garlic cloves, minced

Place onion in a slow cooker. Combine oregano, thyme, garlic powder, salt and pepper; rub over the lamb chops. Place chops over onion. Top with garlic. Cover and cook on low for 4-6 hours or until the meat is tender.

YIELD: 4 SERVINGS.

mushroom pork tenderloin

COOK TIME: 4 TO 5 HOURS

- 2 pork tenderloins (1 pound *each*)
- 1 can (10 3/4 ounces) condensed cream of mushroom soup, undiluted
- 1 can (10 3/4 ounces) condensed golden mushroom soup, undiluted
- 1 can (10 1/2 ounces) condensed French onion soup, undiluted

Hot mashed potatoes, optional

Place pork in a slow cooker. In a bowl, combine the soups; stir until smooth. Pour over pork. Cover and cook on low for 4-5 hours or until the meat is tender. Serve with mashed potatoes if desired.

YIELD: 6 SERVINGS.

Donna Hughes, Rochester, New Hampshire

This moist pork tenderloin in a savory gravy is the best you'll ever taste.
Prepared with canned soups, it couldn't be easier to assemble.

slow cooker salmon loaf

COOK TIME: 4 TO 6 HOURS

 2 eggs, lightly beaten

 2 cups seasoned stuffing croutons

 1 cup chicken broth

 1 cup grated Parmesan cheese

 ¼ teaspoon ground mustard

 1 can (14¾ ounces) salmon, drained, bones and skin removed

1 In a bowl, combine the first five ingredients. Add salmon and mix well. Transfer to a slow cooker coated with nonstick cooking spray. Gently shape the mixture into a loaf.

2 Cover and cook on low for 4-6 hours or until a meat thermometer reads 160°.

YIELD: 6 SERVINGS.

Kelly Ritter, Douglasville, Georgia

I adapted this recipe from one I found in an old slow cooker book of my grandma's. I serve it with macaroni and cheese and pinto beans.

sweet and savory ribs

COOK TIME: 8 TO 9 HOURS

1 large onion, sliced and separated into rings

2½ to 3 pounds boneless country-style pork ribs

1 bottle (18 ounces) honey barbecue sauce

⅓ cup maple syrup

¼ cup spicy brown mustard

½ teaspoon salt

¼ teaspoon pepper

Place onion in a 5-qt. slow cooker. Top with the ribs. Combine the barbecue sauce, syrup, mustard, salt and pepper; pour over ribs. Cover and cook on low for 8-9 hours or until the meat is tender.

YIELD: 6-8 SERVINGS.

Kandy Bingham, Green River, Wyoming

My husband and I love barbecued ribs, but we rarely have time to fire up the grill. So we let the slow cooker do the work for us. By the time we get home from work, the ribs are tender and ready to devour.

pizza in a pot

Anita Doughty, West Des Moines, Iowa

Since most kids will try anything to do with pizza, I rely on this recipe when one of my two teenage sons has a friend stay for dinner. It's frequently a hit.

COOK TIME: 8 TO 9 HOURS

- 1 pound bulk Italian sausage
- 1 can (28 ounces) crushed tomatoes
- 1 can (15½ ounces) chili beans
- 1 can (15 ounces) black beans, rinsed and drained
- 1 can (2¼ ounces) sliced ripe olives, drained
- 1 medium onion, chopped
- 1 small green pepper, chopped
- 2 garlic cloves, minced
- ¼ cup grated Parmesan cheese
- 1 tablespoon quick-cooking tapioca
- 1 tablespoon dried basil
- 1 bay leaf
- 1 teaspoon salt
- ½ teaspoon sugar

Hot cooked pasta

Shredded part-skim mozzarella cheese, optional

1 In a skillet over medium heat, cook the sausage until no longer pink; drain. Transfer to a slow cooker. Add the next 13 ingredients; mix well.

2 Cover and cook on low for 8-9 hours or until slightly thickened. Discard bay leaf. Stir before serving over pasta. Sprinkle with mozzarella cheese if desired.

YIELD: 6-8 SERVINGS.

slow-cooked ham

COOK TIME: 8 TO 10 HOURS

- ½ cup packed brown sugar
- 1 teaspoon ground mustard
- 1 teaspoon prepared horseradish
- 4 tablespoons regular cola, *divided*
- 1 boneless smoked ham (5 to 6 pounds), cut in half

In a bowl, combine the brown sugar, mustard, horseradish and 2 tablespoons cola; mix well. Rub over ham. Place in a 5-qt. slow cooker; pour remaining cola over ham. Cover and cook on low for 8-10 hours or until a meat thermometer reads 140°.

YIELD: 15-20 SERVINGS.

Heather Spring, Sheppard Air Force Base, Texas

Entertaining doesn't get much easier than when you serve this tasty five-ingredient entree.

peachy pork steaks

COOK TIME: 5 HOURS

4 pork steaks (1/2 inch thick), trimmed

2 tablespoons vegetable oil

3/4 teaspoon dried basil

1/4 teaspoon salt

Dash pepper

1 can (15 1/4 ounces) peach slices in heavy syrup, undrained

2 tablespoons cider vinegar

1 tablespoon beef bouillon granules

2 tablespoons cornstarch

1/4 cup cold water

Hot cooked rice

1 In a skillet, brown steaks in oil; sprinkle with basil, salt and pepper. Drain peaches; reserve juice. Place peaches in a slow cooker; top with steaks. Combine reserved juice, vinegar and bouillon; pour over steaks. Cover; cook on high 1 hour. Reduce heat to low and cook 4 hours longer or until meat is tender. Remove steaks and peaches to a serving platter; keep warm.

2 Skim and discard fat from cooking liquid; pour into a saucepan. Combine cornstarch and cold water until smooth; stir into cooking liquid. Bring to a boil; cook and stir 2 minutes. Serve steaks, peaches and sauce over rice.

YIELD: 4 SERVINGS.

Sandra McKenzie, Braham, Minnesota

My mother has been preparing this delicious pork dish for many years.

She always found it a surefire way to get even picky children to eat meat.

It seems that no one can refuse these succulent steaks!

spaghetti pork chops

Ellen Gallavan, Midland, Michigan

In this succulent pork supper, the moist chops simmer to perfection in a tangy sauce, then they are served over pasta.

COOK TIME: 6 TO 8 HOURS

- 3 cans (8 ounces *each*) tomato sauce
- 1 can (10¾ ounces) condensed tomato soup, undiluted
- 1 small onion, finely chopped
- 1 bay leaf
- 1 teaspoon celery seed
- ½ teaspoon Italian seasoning
- 6 bone-in pork chops (1 inch thick)
- 2 tablespoons olive oil

Hot cooked spaghetti

1 In a 5-qt. slow cooker, combine the tomato sauce, soup, onion, bay leaf, celery seed and Italian seasoning. In a large skillet, brown pork chops in oil. Add to the slow cooker.

2 Cover and cook on low for 6-8 hours or until meat is tender. Discard bay leaf. Serve chops and sauce over spaghetti.

YIELD: 6 SERVINGS.

cranberry pork chops

COOK TIME: 7 TO 8 HOURS

6 bone-in pork loin chops

1 can (16 ounces) jellied cranberry sauce

½ cup cranberry *or* apple juice

¼ cup sugar

2 tablespoons spicy brown mustard

2 tablespoons cornstarch

¼ cup cold water

½ teaspoon salt

Dash pepper

1 Place pork chops in a slow cooker. Combine the cranberry sauce, juice, sugar and mustard until smooth; pour over chops. Cover and cook on low for 7-8 hours or until the meat is tender. Remove chops; keep warm.

2 In a saucepan, combine the cornstarch and cold water until smooth; gradually stir in cooking juices. Bring to a boil; cook and stir for 2 minutes or until thickened. Stir in salt and pepper. Serve over chops.

YIELD: 6 SERVINGS.

Robin Czachor, Appleton, Wisconsin

My family raves over these chops. Use the mild sweet-and-sour sauce to make a gravy for mashed potatoes. Add a salad and you have a great meal that didn't keep you in the kitchen for hours.

cranberry pork chops

COOK TIME: 7 TO 8 HOURS

- 6 bone-in pork loin chops
- 1 can (16 ounces) jellied cranberry sauce
- ½ cup cranberry *or* apple juice
- ¼ cup sugar
- 2 tablespoons spicy brown mustard
- 2 tablespoons cornstarch
- ¼ cup cold water
- ½ teaspoon salt

Dash pepper

1 Place pork chops in a slow cooker. Combine the cranberry sauce, juice, sugar and mustard until smooth; pour over chops. Cover and cook on low for 7-8 hours or until the meat is tender. Remove chops; keep warm.

2 In a saucepan, combine the cornstarch and cold water until smooth; gradually stir in cooking juices. Bring to a boil; cook and stir for 2 minutes or until thickened. Stir in salt and pepper. Serve over chops.

YIELD: 6 SERVINGS.

Robin Czachor, Appleton, Wisconsin

My family raves over these chops. Use the mild sweet-and-sour sauce to make a gravy for mashed potatoes. Add a salad and you have a great meal that didn't keep you in the kitchen for hours.

shrimp marinara

COOK TIME: 3½ TO 4½ HOURS

1 can (14½ ounces) Italian diced tomatoes, undrained

1 can (6 ounces) tomato paste

½ to 1 cup water

2 garlic cloves, minced

2 tablespoons minced fresh parsley

1 teaspoon salt, optional

1 teaspoon dried oregano

½ teaspoon dried basil

¼ teaspoon pepper

1 pound fresh *or* frozen shrimp, cooked, peeled and deveined

1 pound spaghetti, cooked and drained

Shredded Parmesan cheese, optional

1 In a slow cooker, combine the first nine ingredients. Cover and cook on low for 3-4 hours.

2 Stir in shrimp. Cover and cook 20 minutes longer or just until shrimp are heated through. Serve over spaghetti. Garnish with Parmesan cheese if desired.

YIELD: 6 SERVINGS.

Sue Mackey, Galesburg, Illinois

I simmer this flavorful marinara sauce for most of the day. Then shortly before mealtime, I simply add cooked shrimp, which merely require being heated through. Served over spaghetti, it makes a delicious dressed-up main dish.

sesame pork roast

COOK TIME: 9 TO 10 HOURS

- 1 boneless pork shoulder roast (4 pounds), trimmed
- 2 cups water
- ½ cup soy sauce
- ¼ cup sesame seeds, toasted
- ¼ cup molasses
- ¼ cup white wine vinegar
- 4 green onions, sliced
- 2 teaspoons garlic powder
- ¼ teaspoon cayenne pepper
- 3 tablespoons cornstarch
- ¼ cup cold water

1 Cut roast in half; place in a large resealable plastic bag or glass dish. In a bowl, combine the water, soy sauce, sesame seeds, molasses, vinegar, onions, garlic powder and cayenne. Pour half over the roast. Cover pork and remaining marinade; refrigerate overnight.

2 Drain pork, discarding marinade. Place roast in a 5-qt. slow cooker; add reserved marinade. Cover; cook on high for 1 hour. Reduce temperature to low; cook 8-9 hours longer or until meat is tender. Remove roast and keep warm. In a saucepan, combine cornstarch and cold water until smooth; stir in cooking juices. Bring to a boil; cook and stir for 2 minutes. Serve with roast.

YIELD: 8 SERVINGS.

Sue Brown, San Miguel, California

I marinate a boneless cut of pork in a tangy sauce overnight before cooking it slowly the next day. The result is a tasty roast that's fall-apart tender.

time to toast?

Toasting sesame seeds brings out a wonderful rich flavor that can complement many recipes and give a bit of crunch to saucy dishes prepared in the slow cooker.

Toast sesame seeds in a dry skillet over medium heat for 10-15 minutes until they're lightly browned, stirring occasionally.

Or, bake them on an ungreased baking sheet at 350° for 10-15 minutes or until they're lightly browned. Watch carefully to avoid scorching.

side dishes & condiments

236

250

Scrumptious side dishes are made even more simple when you use your all-purpose slow cooker! These appealing partners, such as elegant Spiced Acorn Squash (p. 236) and dreamy Creamy Red Potatoes (p. 250), offer delicious new taste twists on old family favorites.

For potlucks, luncheons or large family parties, you'll appreciate the crowd-serving options in this chapter. Best of all, you can make and take your dish to pass in the same pot—and keep it warm throughout mealtime.

lemon red potatoes

COOK TIME: 2½ TO 3 HOURS

1½ pounds medium red potatoes

¼ cup water

¼ cup butter, melted

1 tablespoon lemon juice

3 tablespoons snipped fresh parsley

1 tablespoon snipped fresh chives

Salt and pepper to taste

Cut a strip of peel from around the middle of each potato. Place potatoes and water in a slow cooker. Cover and cook on high for 2½ to 3 hours or until tender (do not overcook); drain. Combine butter, lemon juice, parsley and chives; mix well. Pour over the potatoes and toss to coat. Season with salt and pepper.

YIELD: 6 SERVINGS.

Tara Branham, Cedar Park, Texas

Butter, lemon juice, parsley and chives enhance simple red potatoes. Since they cook in the slow cooker, there's plenty of room on the stove for other dishes.

moist poultry dressing

COOK TIME: 4 TO 5 HOURS

- 2 jars (4½ ounces *each*) sliced mushrooms, drained
- 4 celery ribs, chopped
- 2 medium onions, chopped
- ¼ cup minced fresh parsley
- ¾ cup butter
- 1½ pounds day-old bread, crusts removed and cubed (about 13 cups)
- 1½ teaspoons salt
- 1½ teaspoons rubbed sage
- 1 teaspoon poultry seasoning
- 1 teaspoon dried thyme
- ½ teaspoon pepper
- 2 eggs
- 1 can (14½ ounces) chicken broth

1 In a large skillet, saute the mushrooms, celery, onions and parsley in butter until the vegetables are tender.

2 In a large bowl, toss the bread cubes with salt, sage, poultry seasoning, thyme and pepper. Add the mushroom mixture. Combine eggs and broth; add to the bread mixture and toss. Transfer to a slow cooker.

3 Cover and cook on low for 4-5 hours or until a meat thermometer reads 160°.

YIELD: 12-16 SERVINGS.

Ruth Ann Stelfox, Raymond, Alberta

Tasty mushrooms and onions complement the big herb flavor in this dressing. Every forkful stays wonderfully moist when cooked this way.

vegetable-stuffed peppers

Sandra Allen, Austin, Texas

This recipe came with my slow cooker. I fill green peppers with a flavorful combination of cooked rice, kidney beans, corn and onions. The peppers have become a monthly mainstay for my family.

COOK TIME: 8 HOURS

- 2 cans (14$\frac{1}{2}$ ounces *each*) diced tomatoes, undrained
- 1 can (16 ounces) kidney beans, rinsed and drained
- 1$\frac{1}{2}$ cups cooked rice
- 2 cups (8 ounces) shredded cheddar cheese, *divided*
- 1 package (10 ounces) frozen corn, thawed
- $\frac{1}{4}$ cup chopped onion
- 1 teaspoon Worcestershire sauce
- $\frac{3}{4}$ teaspoon chili powder
- $\frac{1}{2}$ teaspoon pepper
- $\frac{1}{4}$ teaspoon salt
- 6 medium green peppers

1 In a large bowl, combine the tomatoes, beans, rice, 1$\frac{1}{2}$ cups cheese, corn, onion, Worcestershire sauce, chili powder, pepper and salt. Remove and discard tops and seeds of green peppers. Fill each pepper with about 1 cup vegetable mixture. Place in a 5-qt. slow cooker. Cover and cook on low for 8 hours.

2 Sprinkle with remaining cheese. Cover and cook 15 minutes longer or until peppers are tender and cheese is melted.

YIELD: 6 SERVINGS.

michigan beans and sausage

COOK TIME: 6 TO 8 HOURS

1 pound fully cooked kielbasa *or* Polish sausage, halved lengthwise and thinly sliced

1 medium onion, chopped

1 cup ketchup

¾ cup packed brown sugar

½ cup sugar

2 tablespoons vinegar

2 tablespoons molasses

2 tablespoons prepared mustard

3 cans (15½ ounces *each*) great northern beans, rinsed and drained

In a saucepan, cook sausage and onion in boiling water for 2 minutes; drain. In a bowl, combine the ketchup, sugars, vinegar, molasses and mustard. Stir in the beans and sausage mixture. Transfer to a slow cooker. Cover and cook on low for 6-8 hours or until heated through.

YIELD: 14-16 SERVINGS.

Janice Lass, Dorr, Michigan

This recipe from a church cookbook caught my eye years ago. Bean casseroles are a big hit at potlucks and picnics.

cheesy creamed corn

COOK TIME: 4 HOURS

- 3 packages (16 ounces *each*) frozen corn
- 2 packages (one 8 ounces, one 3 ounces) cream cheese, cubed
- ¼ cup butter, cubed
- 3 tablespoons water
- 3 tablespoons milk
- 2 tablespoons sugar
- 6 slices process cheese, cut into small pieces

Combine all ingredients in a slow cooker; mix well. Cover and cook on low for 4 hours or until heated through and the cheese is melted. Stir well before serving.

YIELD: 12 SERVINGS.

Mary Ann Truit, Wichita, Kansas

My family really likes this creamy, cheesy side dish—and it's so easy to make. Even those who usually don't eat much corn will ask for a second helping.

slow-simmered kidney beans

COOK TIME: 6 TO 8 HOURS

6 bacon strips, diced

½ pound fully cooked kielbasa *or* Polish sausage, chopped

4 cans (16 ounces *each*) kidney beans, rinsed and drained

1 can (28 ounces) diced tomatoes, drained

2 medium sweet red peppers, chopped

1 large onion, chopped

1 cup ketchup

½ cup packed brown sugar

¼ cup honey

¼ cup molasses

1 tablespoon Worcestershire sauce

1 teaspoon salt

1 teaspoon ground mustard

2 medium unpeeled red apples, cored and cut into ½-inch pieces

1 In a skillet, cook bacon until crisp. Remove with a slotted spoon to paper towels. Add sausage to drippings; cook and stir 5 minutes. Drain; set aside.

2 In an ungreased 5-qt. slow cooker, combine the beans, tomatoes, red peppers, onion, ketchup, brown sugar, honey, molasses, Worcestershire sauce, salt and mustard. Stir in the bacon and sausage.

3 Cover and cook on low for 4-6 hours. Stir in the apples. Cover and cook 2 hours longer or until bubbly.

YIELD: 16 SERVINGS.

Sheila Vail, Long Beach, California

My husband always puts us down for this side dish when we're invited to a potluck. Canned beans cut down on prep time yet get plenty of zip from bacon, apple, red pepper and onion. I like simmering this mixture in the slow cooker because it blends the flavors and I don't have to stand over the stove.

slow-cooked sage dressing

COOK TIME: 4 TO 5 HOURS

14 to 15 cups day-old bread cubes

3 cups chopped celery

1½ cups chopped onion

1½ teaspoons rubbed sage

1 teaspoon salt

½ teaspoon pepper

1¼ cups butter, melted

Combine bread, celery, onion, sage, salt and pepper; mix well. Add butter and toss. Spoon into a 5-qt. slow cooker. Cover and cook on low for 4-5 hours, stirring once.

YIELD: ABOUT 12 SERVINGS.

Ellen Benninger, Stoneboro, Pennsylvania

This recipe is such a help at holiday time. There's room in the oven for other dishes when this simple yet delicious dressing is fixed in the slow cooker.

potato hot dish

COOK TIME: 8 TO 10 HOURS

6 medium potatoes, peeled and cut into ¼-inch strips

2 cups (8 ounces) shredded cheddar cheese

1 can (10¾ ounces) condensed cream of chicken soup, undiluted

1 small onion, chopped *or* 1 tablespoon dried minced onion

7 tablespoons butter, melted, *divided*

1 teaspoon salt

1 teaspoon pepper

1 cup (8 ounces) sour cream

2 cups seasoned stuffing cubes

1 Toss the potatoes and cheese; place in a 5-qt. slow cooker. Combine soup, onion, 4 tablespoons butter, salt and pepper; pour over potato mixture.

2 Cover and cook on low for 8-10 hours or until potatoes are tender. Stir in sour cream. Toss stuffing cubes and remaining butter; sprinkle over potatoes.

YIELD: 10-12 SERVINGS.

Melissa Marzolf, Marysville, Michigan

For a comforting side dish that feeds a crowd, try these saucy, slow-cooked potatoes. A topping of buttered croutons covers the creamy combination.

spiced acorn squash

Carol Greco, Centereach, New York

Working full time, I found I didn't always have time to cook the meals my family loved. So I re-created many of our favorites in the slow cooker. This cinnamony treatment for squash is one of them.

COOK TIME: 4 HOURS

- ¾ cup packed brown sugar
- 1 teaspoon ground cinnamon
- 1 teaspoon ground nutmeg
- 2 small acorn squash, halved and seeded
- ¾ cup raisins
- 4 tablespoons butter
- ½ cup water

1 Combine brown sugar, cinnamon and nutmeg; spoon into the squash halves. Sprinkle with raisins. Top each with 1 tablespoon of butter. Wrap each squash half individually in heavy-duty foil; seal tightly. Pour water into a slow cooker. Place the squash, cut side up, in slow cooker (packets may be stacked).

2 Cover and cook on high for 4 hours or until the squash is tender. Open foil packets carefully to allow steam to escape.

YIELD: 4 SERVINGS.

hot fruit salad

COOK TIME: 3 TO 4 HOURS

- 1 jar (25 ounces) chunky applesauce
- 1 can (21 ounces) cherry pie filling
- 1 can (20 ounces) pineapple chunks, undrained
- 1 can (15¼ ounces) sliced peaches, undrained
- 1 can (15¼ ounces) apricot halves, undrained
- 1 can (15 ounces) mandarin oranges, undrained
- ½ cup packed brown sugar
- 1 teaspoon ground cinnamon

Place the first six ingredients in a slow cooker and stir gently. Combine brown sugar and cinnamon; sprinkle over fruit mixture. Cover and cook on low for 3-4 hours.

YIELD: 16 SERVINGS.

Barb Vande Voort, New Sharon, Iowa

This spicy fruit mixture is a breeze to make—just open the cans and empty them into the slow cooker. With its pretty color from cherry pie filling, this salad is nice for any special occasion.

vegetable medley

COOK TIME: 5 TO 6 HOURS

    4 cups diced peeled potatoes

1½ cups frozen whole kernel corn *or*
      1 can (15¼ ounces) whole kernel
      corn, drained

    4 medium tomatoes, seeded and
      diced

    1 cup sliced carrots

  ½ cup chopped onion

  ¾ teaspoon salt

  ½ teaspoon sugar

  ½ teaspoon dill weed

  ⅛ teaspoon pepper

In a slow cooker, combine all ingredients. Cover; cook on low for 5-6 hours or until vegetables are tender.

YIELD: 8 SERVINGS.

Terry Maly, Olathe, Kansas

This is a wonderful side dish to make when garden vegetables are plentiful. The colorful combination is a great complement to any entree.

chunky applesauce

COOK TIME: 6 TO 8 HOURS

- 8 to 10 large tart apples, peeled and cut into chunks
- ½ to 1 cup sugar
- ½ cup water
- 1 teaspoon ground cinnamon

Combine apples, sugar, water and cinnamon in a slow cooker; stir gently. Cover and cook on low for 6-8 hours or until apples are tender.

YIELD: 5 CUPS.

Lisa Roessner, Ft. Recovery, Ohio

I'm so glad my mother gave me the recipe for this warm and cinnamony apple dish. Simmering it in a slow cooker fills the house with a wonderful aroma.

hot german potato salad

COOK TIME: 4 TO 5 HOURS

- 8 medium potatoes, peeled and cut into ¼-inch slices
- 2 celery ribs, chopped
- 1 large onion, chopped
- 1 cup water
- ⅔ cup cider vinegar
- ⅓ cup sugar
- 2 tablespoons quick-cooking tapioca
- 1 teaspoon salt
- ¾ teaspoon celery seed
- ¼ teaspoon pepper
- 6 bacon strips, cooked and crumbled
- ¼ cup minced fresh parsley

1 In a slow cooker, combine the potatoes, celery and onion. In a bowl, combine the water, vinegar, sugar, tapioca, salt, celery seed and pepper. Pour over the potatoes; stir gently to coat.

2 Cover and cook on high for 4-5 hours or until potatoes are tender. Just before serving, sprinkle with bacon and parsley.

YIELD: 8-10 SERVINGS.

Marlene Muckenhirn, Delano, Minnesota

I make this zesty salad with potatoes, celery and onion. It's a terrific side dish when served warm with crumbled bacon and fresh parsley sprinkled on top.

spanish hominy

Donna Brockett, Kingfisher, Oklahoma

I received this recipe from a good friend who is known to be a fabulous cook. The colorful side dish gets its zesty flavor from spicy canned tomatoes with green chilies. It's a great way to perk up any main dish.

COOK TIME: 6 TO 8 HOURS

- 4 cans (15½ ounces *each*) hominy, drained
- 1 can (14½ ounces) diced tomatoes, undrained
- 1 can (10 ounces) diced tomatoes and green chilies, undrained
- 1 can (8 ounces) tomato sauce
- ¾ pound sliced bacon, diced
- 1 large onion, chopped
- 1 medium green pepper, chopped

1 In a slow cooker, combine the hominy, tomatoes and tomato sauce. In a skillet, cook the bacon until crisp; remove with a slotted spoon to paper towels. Drain, reserving 1 tablespoon drippings.

2 Saute the onion and green pepper in the drippings until tender. Stir onion mixture and bacon into the hominy mixture. Cover; cook on low for 6-8 hours or until heated through.

YIELD: 12 SERVINGS.

partytime beans

COOK TIME: 5 TO 7 HOURS

1½ cups ketchup

1 medium onion, chopped

1 medium green pepper, chopped

1 medium sweet red pepper, chopped

½ cup water

½ cup packed brown sugar

2 bay leaves

2 to 3 teaspoons cider vinegar

1 teaspoon ground mustard

⅛ teaspoon pepper

1 can (16 ounces) kidney beans, rinsed and drained

1 can (15½ ounces) great northern beans, rinsed and drained

1 can (15 ounces) lima beans, rinsed and drained

1 can (15 ounces) black beans, rinsed and drained

1 can (15½ ounces) black-eyed peas, rinsed and drained

In a slow cooker, combine the first 10 ingredients; mix well. Add the beans and peas; mix well. Cover and cook on low for 5-7 hours or until onion and peppers are tender. Remove bay leaves.

YIELD: 14-16 SERVINGS.

Jean Cantner, Boston, Virginia

A friend brought this colorful bean dish to my house for a church circle potluck dinner. As soon as I tasted these slightly sweet baked beans, I had to have the recipe. I've served this and shared the recipe many times since.

cheesy hash brown potatoes

COOK TIME: 4 TO 4½ HOURS

2 cans (10¾ ounces *each*) condensed cheddar cheese soup, undiluted

1⅓ cups buttermilk

2 tablespoons butter, melted

½ teaspoon seasoned salt

¼ teaspoon garlic powder

¼ teaspoon pepper

1 package (2 pounds) frozen cubed hash brown potatoes

¼ cup grated Parmesan cheese

1 teaspoon paprika

In a slow cooker, combine the first six ingredients; stir in hash browns. Sprinkle with Parmesan cheese and paprika. Cover and cook on low for 4 to 4½ hours or until potatoes are tender.

YIELD: 6-8 SERVINGS.

Becky Weseman, Becker, Minnesota

I adapted this recipe for my slow cooker so I could bring these cheesy potatoes to a potluck picnic. Canned soup and frozen hash browns make this dish easy to assemble.

lazy-day cranberry relish

COOK TIME: 6 HOURS

2 cups sugar

1 cup orange juice

1 teaspoon grated orange peel

4 cups fresh *or* frozen cranberries

In a slow cooker, combine sugar, orange juice and peel; stir until sugar is dissolved. Add the cranberries. Cover and cook on low for 6 hours. Mash the mixture. Chill several hours or overnight.

YIELD: 10-12 SERVINGS (3 CUPS).

June Formanek, Belle Plaine, Iowa

When I get busy with holiday bustle, this no-fuss, ruby-red condiment can be simmering in my kitchen.

four-bean medley

COOK TIME: 6 TO 7 HOURS

  8 bacon strips, diced

  2 medium onions, quartered and sliced

  ¾ cup packed brown sugar

  ½ cup vinegar

  1 teaspoon salt

  1 teaspoon ground mustard

  ½ teaspoon garlic powder

  1 can (16 ounces) baked beans, undrained

  1 can (16 ounces) kidney beans, rinsed and drained

  1 can (15½ ounces) butter beans, rinsed and drained

  1 can (14½ ounces) cut green beans, drained

1 In a skillet, cook bacon until crisp. Drain, reserving 2 tablespoons drippings; set bacon aside. Saute onions in drippings until tender. Stir in brown sugar, vinegar, salt, mustard and garlic powder. Simmer, uncovered, for 15 minutes or until the onions are golden brown.

2 Combine the beans in a slow cooker. Add onion mixture and bacon; mix well. Cover and cook on low for 6-7 hours or until the beans are tender. Serve with a slotted spoon.

YIELD: 8-10 SERVINGS.

Susanne Wasson, Montgomery, New York

This bean side dish will draw compliments. It's a hearty and great-tasting addition to any meal. Because it's easy to fix ahead and simmer in the slow cooker, it's convenient to take to potluck dinners and church meals.

mushroom wild rice

COOK TIME: 7 TO 8 HOURS

2¼ cups water

1 can (10½ ounces) condensed beef consomme, undiluted

1 can (10½ ounces) condensed French onion soup, undiluted

3 cans (4 ounces *each*) mushroom stems and pieces, drained

½ cup butter, melted

1 cup uncooked brown rice

1 cup uncooked wild rice

In a slow cooker, combine all ingredients; stir well. Cover and cook on low for 7-8 hours or until rice is tender.

YIELD: 12-16 SERVINGS.

Bob Malchow, Monon, Indiana

This is one of my favorite recipes from my mother. With only seven ingredients, it's quick to assemble in the morning before I leave for work.

sweet potato stuffing

Kelly Pollock, London, Ontario

Mom likes to make sure there will be enough stuffing to satisfy our large family. For our holiday gatherings, she slow-cooks this tasty sweet potato dressing in addition to the traditional stuffing cooked inside the turkey.

COOK TIME: 4 HOURS

- ½ cup chopped celery
- ½ cup chopped onion
- ¼ cup butter
- 6 cups dry bread cubes
- 1 large sweet potato, cooked, peeled and finely chopped
- ½ cup chicken broth
- ¼ cup chopped pecans
- ½ teaspoon poultry seasoning
- ½ teaspoon rubbed sage
- ½ teaspoon salt
- ½ teaspoon pepper

In a skillet, saute celery and onion in butter until tender. Add remaining ingredients; toss gently. Transfer to a greased slow cooker. Cover and cook on low for 4 hours or until bread and vegetables are soft.

YIELD: 10 SERVINGS.

creamy red potatoes

COOK TIME: 8 HOURS

- 2 pounds small red potatoes, quartered
- 1 package (8 ounces) cream cheese, softened
- 1 can (10¾ ounces) condensed cream of potato soup, undiluted
- 1 envelope ranch salad dressing mix

Place potatoes in a 3-qt. slow cooker. In a small mixing bowl, beat cream cheese, soup and salad dressing mix until blended. Stir into potatoes. Cover and cook on low for 8 hours or until potatoes are tender.

YIELD: 4-6 SERVINGS.

Shelia Schmitt, Topeka, Kansas

I can please a crowd with this rich and creamy side dish. It's easy to double, and I always receive compliments when I take it to potlucks.

slow-cooked vegetables

COOK TIME: 7 TO 8 HOURS

- 4 celery ribs, cut into 1-inch pieces
- 4 small carrots, cut into 1-inch pieces
- 2 medium tomatoes, cut into chunks
- 2 medium onions, thinly sliced
- 2 cups cut fresh green beans (1-inch pieces)
- 1 medium green pepper, cut into 1-inch pieces
- ¼ cup butter, melted
- 3 tablespoons quick-cooking tapioca
- 1 tablespoon sugar
- 2 teaspoons salt
- ⅛ teaspoon pepper

Place the vegetables in a slow cooker. Combine butter, tapioca, sugar, salt and pepper; pour over vegetables and stir well. Cover and cook on low for 7-8 hours or until vegetables are tender. Serve with a slotted spoon.

YIELD: 8 SERVINGS.

Kathy Westendorf, Westgate, Iowa

I simmer a variety of garden-fresh vegetables into this satisfying side dish. My sister-in-law shared this recipe with me. It's a favorite at holiday gatherings and potlucks.

marmalade-glazed carrots

COOK TIME: 5½ TO 6½ HOURS

- 1 package (2 pounds) fresh baby carrots
- ½ cup orange marmalade
- 3 tablespoons cold water, *divided*
- 2 tablespoons brown sugar
- 1 tablespoon butter, melted
- ½ teaspoon ground cinnamon
- ¼ teaspoon salt
- ¼ teaspoon ground nutmeg
- ⅛ teaspoon pepper
- 1 tablespoon cornstarch

1 In a 3-qt. slow cooker, combine the carrots, marmalade, 1 tablespoon water, brown sugar, butter and seasonings. Cover and cook on low for 5-6 hours or until carrots are tender.

2 Combine cornstarch and remaining water until smooth; stir into carrot mixture. Cover and cook on high for 30 minutes or until thickened. Serve with a slotted spoon.

YIELD: 6 SERVINGS.

Barb Rudyk, Vermilion, Alberta

This side dish is ideal when you'd like to serve your vegetables in a different way for a special dinner. Cinnamon and nutmeg season baby carrots that are simmered with orange marmalade and brown sugar.

cheesy spinach

COOK TIME: 5 TO 6 HOURS

- 2 packages (10 ounces *each*) frozen chopped spinach, thawed and well drained
- 2 cups (16 ounces) small-curd cottage cheese
- 1½ cups cubed process cheese (Velveeta)
- 3 eggs, lightly beaten
- ¼ cup butter, cubed
- ¼ cup all-purpose flour
- 1 teaspoon salt

In a large bowl, combine all ingredients. Pour into a greased slow cooker. Cover and cook on high for 1 hour. Reduce heat to low; cook 4-5 hours longer or until a knife inserted near the center comes out clean.

YIELD: 6-8 SERVINGS.

Frances Moore, Decatur, Illinois

My daughter often serves this cheese and spinach blend at church suppers. She always comes home with an empty slow cooker. Everyone likes this flavorful combination once they try it.

barbecued beans

Diane Hixon, Niceville, Florida

Most members of my family would agree that no picnic is complete until these delicious beans have made their appearance. Preparing them in a slow cooker makes them easy to transport to any gathering.

COOK TIME: 10 TO 12 HOURS

- 1 **pound dried navy beans**
- 1 **pound sliced bacon, cooked and crumbled**
- 1 **bottle (32 ounces) tomato juice**
- 1 **can (8 ounces) tomato sauce**
- 2 **cups chopped onion**
- 2/3 **cup packed brown sugar**
- 1 **tablespoon soy sauce**
- 2 **teaspoons garlic salt**
- 1 **teaspoon Worcestershire sauce**
- 1 **teaspoon ground mustard**

1 Place beans in a 3-qt. saucepan; cover with water. Bring to a boil; boil for 2 minutes. Remove from the heat; let stand for 1 hour. Drain beans and discard liquid.

2 In a 5-qt. slow cooker, combine all of the remaining ingredients; mix well. Add the beans. Cover and cook on high for 2 hours. Reduce heat to low and cook 8-10 hours longer or until beans are tender.

YIELD: 12-15 servings.

simple saucy potatoes

COOK TIME: 4 TO 5 HOURS

4 cans (15 ounces *each*) sliced white potatoes, drained

2 cans (10¾ ounces *each*) condensed cream of celery soup, undiluted

2 cups (16 ounces) sour cream

10 bacon strips, cooked and crumbled

6 green onions, thinly sliced

Place potatoes in a slow cooker. Combine the remaining ingredients; pour over potatoes and mix well. Cover and cook on high for 4-5 hours.

YIELD: 12 SERVINGS.

Gloria Schroeder, Ottawa Lake, Michigan

These rich and creamy potatoes are easy to prepare for potlucks and holiday meals. This saucy side dish always gets rave reviews wherever I take it.

all-day apple butter

COOK TIME: 11 TO 13 HOURS

5½ pounds apples, peeled and finely chopped

4 cups sugar

2 to 3 teaspoons ground cinnamon

¼ teaspoon ground cloves

¼ teaspoon salt

1 Place apples in a slow cooker. Combine sugar, cinnamon, cloves and salt; pour over apples and mix well. Cover and cook on high for 1 hour. Reduce heat to low; cover and cook for 9-11 hours or until thickened and dark brown, stirring occasionally (stir more frequently as it thickens to prevent sticking).

2 Uncover and cook on low 1 hour longer. If desired, stir with a wire whisk until smooth. Spoon into freezer containers, leaving ½-in. headspace. Cover and refrigerate or freeze.

YIELD: 4 PINTS.

Betty Ruenholl, Syracuse, Nebraska

With this spread, the fresh flavor of apples at harvesttime can be enjoyed all year. Depending on the sweetness of the apples used, you can adjust the sugar to taste.

slow-cooked beans

COOK TIME: 2 HOURS

  4 cans (15½ ounces *each*) great northern beans, rinsed and drained

  4 cans (15 ounces *each*) black beans, rinsed and drained

  2 cans (15 ounces *each*) butter beans, rinsed and drained

2¼ cups barbecue sauce

2¼ cups salsa

 ¾ cup packed brown sugar

 ½ to 1 teaspoon hot pepper sauce

In a 5-qt. slow cooker, gently combine all ingredients. Cover and cook on low for 2 hours or until heated through.

YIELD: 16 SERVINGS.

Joy Beck, Cincinnati, Ohio

This flavorful bean dish adds nice variety to any buffet. It's different from more traditional baked beans. It's a snap to prepare, too.

sweet 'n' sour beans

COOK TIME: 3 TO 4 HOURS

- 8 bacon strips, diced
- 2 medium onions, halved and thinly sliced
- 1 cup packed brown sugar
- ½ cup cider vinegar
- 1 teaspoon salt
- 1 teaspoon ground mustard
- ½ teaspoon garlic powder
- 1 can (28 ounces) baked beans, undrained
- 1 can (16 ounces) kidney beans, rinsed and drained
- 1 can (15½ ounces) pinto beans, rinsed and drained
- 1 can (15 ounces) lima beans, rinsed and drained
- 1 can (15½ ounces) black-eyed peas, rinsed and drained

1 In a large skillet, cook bacon until crisp. Remove to paper towels. Drain, reserving 2 tablespoons drippings. In the drippings, saute onions until tender. Add brown sugar, vinegar, salt, mustard and garlic powder. Bring to a boil.

2 In a slow cooker, combine beans and peas. Add onion mixture and bacon; mix well. Cover and cook on high for 3-4 hours or until heated through.

YIELD: 15-20 SERVINGS.

Barbara Short, Mena, Arkansas

This recipe is popular on both sides of the border. It came from a friend in Alaska, then traveled with me to Mexico, where I lived for 5 years, and is now a potluck favorite in my Arkansas community. It's easy to keep the beans warm and serve from a slow cooker.

sweet endings

274

277

A quick and easy meal doesn't have to end with the main course. Turn on your slow cooker for dessert, too, and serve puddings, cobblers, cakes, fruits or fondues as your final course!

Delight your family with sweet concoctions like Hot Caramel Apples (p. 277)—a delicious complement to any meal. Or discover super kitchen shortcuts with the time-saving, tummy-tempting candy, Easy Chocolate Clusters (p. 274).

pumpkin pie pudding

COOK TIME: 6 TO 7 HOURS

    1 can (15 ounces) solid-pack pumpkin

    1 can (12 ounces) evaporated milk

    ¾ cup sugar

    ½ cup biscuit/baking mix

    2 eggs, beaten

    2 tablespoons butter, melted

  2½ teaspoons pumpkin pie spice

    2 teaspoons vanilla extract

Whipped topping, optional

1 In a large bowl, combine the first eight ingredients. Transfer to a slow cooker coated with nonstick cooking spray.

2 Cover and cook on low for 6-7 hours or until a thermometer reads 160°. Serve in bowls with whipped topping if desired.

YIELD: 6-8 SERVINGS.

Andrea Schaak, Bloomington, Minnesota

My husband loves anything pumpkin, and this creamy, comforting dessert is one of his favorites. We make this super-easy pudding year-round, but it's especially nice in fall.

black and blue cobbler

COOK TIME: 2 TO 2½ HOURS

1 cup all-purpose flour

1½ cups sugar, *divided*

1 teaspoon baking powder

¼ teaspoon salt

¼ teaspoon ground cinnamon

¼ teaspoon ground nutmeg

2 eggs, beaten

2 tablespoons milk

2 tablespoons vegetable oil

2 cups fresh *or* frozen blackberries

2 cups fresh *or* frozen blueberries

¾ cup water

1 teaspoon grated orange peel

Whipped cream *or* ice cream, optional

1 In a bowl, combine flour, ¾ cup sugar, baking powder, salt, cinnamon and nutmeg. Combine eggs, milk and oil; stir into dry ingredients just until moistened. Spread the batter evenly onto the bottom of a greased 5-qt. slow cooker. In a saucepan, combine berries, water, orange peel and remaining sugar; bring to a boil. Remove from the heat; immediately pour over batter.

2 Cover and cook on high for 2 to 2½ hours or until a toothpick inserted into the batter comes out clean. Turn cooker off. Uncover and let stand for 30 minutes before serving. Serve with whipped cream or ice cream if desired.

YIELD: 6 SERVINGS.

Martha Creveling, Orlando, Florida

One day, I decided to try my favorite fruity dessert recipe in the slow cooker. It took a bit of experimenting, but the results are "berry" well worth it.

minister's delight

Mary Ann Potte, Blue Springs, Missouri

A friend gave me this recipe. She said a local minister's wife fixed it every Sunday, so she named it accordingly.

COOK TIME: 2 TO 3 HOURS

- 1 can (21 ounces) cherry *or* apple pie filling
- 1 package (18¼ ounces) yellow cake mix
- ½ cup butter, melted
- ⅓ cup chopped walnuts, optional

Place pie filling in a slow cooker. Combine dry cake mix and butter (mixture will be crumbly); sprinkle over filling. Sprinkle with walnuts if desired. Cover and cook on low for 2-3 hours. Serve in bowls.

YIELD: 10-12 SERVINGS.

chocolate pudding cake

COOK TIME: 6 TO 7 HOURS

- 1 package (18¼ ounces) chocolate cake mix
- 1 package (3.9 ounces) instant chocolate pudding mix
- 2 cups (16 ounces) sour cream
- 4 eggs
- 1 cup water
- ¾ cup vegetable oil
- 1 cup (6 ounces) semisweet chocolate chips

Whipped cream *or* ice cream, optional

1 In a mixing bowl, combine the first six ingredients. Beat on medium speed for 2 minutes. Stir in chocolate chips. Pour into a 5-qt. slow cooker coated with nonstick cooking spray.

2 Cover and cook on low for 6-7 hours or until a toothpick inserted near the center comes out with moist crumbs. Serve in bowls with whipped cream or ice cream if desired.

YIELD: 10-12 SERVINGS.

Paige Arnette, Lawrenceville, Georgia

This recipe makes a rich, fudgy dessert that's a cross between pudding and cake. I like to serve this scrumptious treat warm with a scoop of vanilla ice cream. Whenever I take it to parties, everybody wants the recipe.

warm strawberry fondue

COOK TIME: SERVE IN SLOW COOKER

1 package (10 ounces) frozen
   sweetened sliced strawberries,
   thawed

¼ cup half-and-half cream

1 teaspoon cornstarch

½ teaspoon lemon juice

Angel food cake cubes and fresh fruit

1 In a food processor or blender, combine the strawberries, cream, cornstarch and lemon juice; cover and process until smooth.

2 Pour into a saucepan. Bring to a boil; cook and stir for 2 minutes or until slightly thickened. Transfer to a fondue pot or mini slow cooker; keep warm. Serve with cake and fruit.

YIELD: 1½ CUPS.

Sharon Mensing, Greenfield, Iowa

You need only a handful of ingredients to fix this unusual fruit fondue.

Use grapes, bananas, strawberries and angel food cake as dippers.

fruit dessert topping

COOK TIME: 3½ TO 4½ HOURS

3 medium tart apples, peeled and sliced

3 medium pears, peeled and sliced

1 tablespoon lemon juice

½ cup packed brown sugar

½ cup maple syrup

¼ cup butter, melted

½ cup chopped pecans

¼ cup raisins

2 cinnamon sticks (3 inches)

1 tablespoon cornstarch

2 tablespoons cold water

Pound cake *or* ice cream

1 In a slow cooker, toss the apples and pears with the lemon juice. Combine the brown sugar, maple syrup and butter; pour over fruit. Stir in the pecans, raisins and cinnamon sticks. Cover and cook on low for 3-4 hours.

2 Combine the cornstarch and water until smooth; gradually stir into slow cooker. Cover and cook on high for 30-40 minutes or until thickened. Discard cinnamon sticks. Serve over pound cake or ice cream.

YIELD: ABOUT 6 CUPS.

Doris Heath, Franklin, North Carolina

You'll quickly warm up to the down-home flavor of this fruit topping. Spoon it over vanilla ice cream or slices of pound cake.

raisin bread pudding

COOK TIME: 4 TO 5 HOURS

  8 slices bread, cubed

  4 eggs

  2 cups milk

  ¼ cup sugar

  ¼ cup butter, melted

  ¼ cup raisins

  ½ teaspoon ground cinnamon

SAUCE:

  2 tablespoons butter

  2 tablespoons all-purpose flour

  1 cup water

  ¾ cup sugar

  1 teaspoon vanilla extract

1 Place the bread cubes in a greased slow cooker. In a bowl, beat the eggs and milk; stir in the sugar, butter, raisins and cinnamon. Pour over the bread cubes; stir. Cover and cook on high for 1 hour. Reduce heat to low; cook for 3-4 hours or until a thermometer reads 160°.

2 Just before serving, melt the butter in a saucepan. Stir in flour until smooth. Gradually add the water, sugar and vanilla. Bring to a boil; cook and stir for 2 minutes or until thickened. Serve with warm bread pudding.

YIELD: 6 SERVINGS.

Sherry Niese, McComb, Ohio

My sister gave me the recipe for this delicious bread pudding that's dotted with raisins. It's a big hit with everyone who's tried it. A home-made vanilla sauce goes together quickly on the stovetop and is yummy drizzled over warm servings of this old-fashioned-tasting treat.

nutty apple streusel dessert

COOK TIME: 6 TO 7 HOURS

   6 cups sliced peeled tart apples

1¼ teaspoons ground cinnamon

   ¼ teaspoon ground allspice

   ¼ teaspoon ground nutmeg

   ¾ cup milk

   2 tablespoons butter, softened

   ¾ cup sugar

   2 eggs

   1 teaspoon vanilla extract

   ½ cup biscuit/baking mix

TOPPING:

   1 cup biscuit/baking mix

   ⅓ cup packed brown sugar

   3 tablespoons cold butter

   ½ cup sliced almonds

Ice cream *or* whipped cream, optional

Jacki Every, Rotterdam, New York

Many people don't think of using a slow cooker to make dessert, but I like finishing up our dinner and having this hot, scrumptious apple treat waiting to be served up. I can start it in the morning and not think about it all day.

1 In a large bowl, toss apples with cinnamon, allspice and nutmeg. Place in a greased slow cooker. In a mixing bowl, combine milk, butter, sugar, eggs, vanilla and baking mix; mix well. Spoon over apples.

2 For topping, combine the biscuit mix and brown sugar in a bowl; cut in butter until crumbly. Add almonds; sprinkle over the apples.

3 Cover and cook on low for 6-7 hours or until the apples are tender. Serve with ice cream or whipped cream if desired.

YIELD: 6-8 SERVINGS.

fruit compote dessert

Laura Bryant German, West Warren, Massachusetts

This is one of the first desserts I learned to make in the slow cooker, and it's the one guests still enjoy most. It tastes like it came from a fancy restaurant.

COOK TIME: 3 TO 4 HOURS

- 2 medium tart apples, peeled
- 2 medium fresh peaches, peeled and cubed
- 2 cups unsweetened pineapple chunks
- 1¼ cups unsweetened pineapple juice
- ¼ cup honey
- 2 lemon slices (¼ inch)
- 1 cinnamon stick (3½ inches)
- 1 medium firm banana, thinly sliced

Whipped cream, sliced almonds and maraschino cherries, optional

1 Cut apples into ¼-in. slices and then in half; place in a slow cooker. Add the peaches, pineapple, pineapple juice, honey, lemon and cinnamon.

2 Cover and cook on low for 3-4 hours. Just before serving, stir in the banana slices. Serve with a slotted spoon if desired. Garnish with whipped cream, almonds and cherries if desired.

YIELD: 8 SERVINGS.

apple-nut bread pudding

COOK TIME: 3 TO 4 HOURS

  8 slices raisin bread, cubed

  2 medium tart apples, peeled and sliced

  1 cup chopped pecans, toasted

  1 cup sugar

  1 teaspoon ground cinnamon

½ teaspoon ground nutmeg

  3 eggs, lightly beaten

  2 cups half-and-half cream

¼ cup apple juice

¼ cup butter, melted

Vanilla ice cream

1 Place bread cubes, apples and pecans in a greased slow cooker. In a bowl, combine the sugar, cinnamon and nutmeg. Add the eggs, cream, apple juice and butter; mix well. Pour over the bread mixture.

2 Cover and cook on low for 3-4 hours or until a knife inserted in the center comes out clean. Serve with ice cream.

YIELD: 6-8 SERVINGS.

Lori Fox, Menomonee Falls, Wisconsin

Traditional bread pudding gives way to autumn's influences in this comforting dessert. I add apples and pecans to this slow-cooked recipe, then top warm servings with ice cream.

strawberry rhubarb sauce

COOK TIME: 6 TO 7 HOURS

  6 cups chopped rhubarb (½-inch pieces)

  1 cup sugar

  ½ teaspoon grated orange peel

  ½ teaspoon ground ginger

  1 cinnamon stick (3 inches)

  ½ cup white grape juice

  2 cups halved unsweetened strawberries

Pound cake *or* vanilla ice cream

1 Place rhubarb in a slow cooker. Combine sugar, orange peel and ginger; sprinkle over rhubarb. Add cinnamon stick and grape juice.

2 Cover and cook on low for 5-6 hours or until rhubarb is tender. Stir in strawberries; cook 1 hour longer. Discard cinnamon stick. Serve over cake or ice cream.

YIELD: 10 SERVINGS.

Judith Waxman, Washington, D.C.

This tart and tangy fruit sauce is excellent over pound cake or ice cream. I've served the rosy-colored mixture many times and received rave reviews from friends and family.

butterscotch fondue

COOK TIME: SERVE IN SLOW COOKER

- ½ cup butter, cubed
- 2 cups packed brown sugar
- 1 can (14 ounces) sweetened condensed milk
- 1 cup light corn syrup
- 2 tablespoons water
- ¼ cup English toffee bits *or* almond brickle chips
- 1 teaspoon vanilla extract

Angel food cake cubes and fresh fruit

1 In a large saucepan, combine the butter, brown sugar, milk, corn syrup and water. Cook and stir over medium heat until smooth. Remove from the heat. Stir in toffee bits and vanilla.

2 Transfer to a fondue pot or mini slow cooker; keep warm. Serve with cake and fruit.

YIELD: 4 CUPS.

Taste of Home Test Kitchen, Greendale, Wisconsin

Folks of all ages will enjoy dipping into a pot filled with this yummy concoction. The combination of brown sugar, sweetened condensed milk and toffee bits has lovely flavor.

chocolate bread pudding

COOK TIME: 2¼ TO 2½ HOURS

- 6 cups cubed day-old bread (¾-inch cubes)
- 1½ cups semisweet chocolate chips
- 1 cup fresh raspberries
- 4 eggs
- ½ cup heavy whipping cream
- ½ cup milk
- ¼ cup sugar
- 1 teaspoon vanilla extract

Whipped cream and additional raspberries, optional

1 In a greased slow cooker, layer half of the bread cubes, chocolate chips and raspberries. Repeat layers. In a bowl, whisk the eggs, cream, milk, sugar and vanilla. Pour over bread mixture.

2 Cover and cook on high for 2¼ to 2½ hours or until a thermometer reads 160°. Let stand for 5-10 minutes. Serve with whipped cream and additional raspberries if desired.

YIELD: 6-8 SERVINGS.

Becky Foster, Union, Oregon

I love chocolate and I love berries, so I was thrilled to come across a recipe that combines the two. I like to use egg bread when making this dessert. Since it cooks in the slow cooker, I can tend to other things.

easy chocolate clusters

Doris Reynolds, Munds Park, Arizona

Use this simple recipe to make a big batch of chocolate candy without a lot of fuss. I've sent these clusters to my husband's office a number of times…and passed the recipe along as well.

COOK TIME: 2 HOURS

- 2 pounds white candy coating, broken into small pieces
- 2 cups (12 ounces) semisweet chocolate chips
- 1 package (4 ounces) German sweet chocolate
- 1 jar (24 ounces) dry roasted peanuts

1 In a slow cooker, combine candy coating, chocolate chips and German chocolate. Cover and cook on high for 1 hour. Reduce heat to low; cover and cook 1 hour longer or until melted, stirring every 15 minutes. Add peanuts; mix well.

2 Drop by teaspoonfuls onto waxed paper. Let stand until set. Store at room temperature.

YIELD: 3½ DOZEN.

warm apple delight

COOK TIME: 3 HOURS

- 8 medium tart apples (about 3½ pounds), peeled and sliced
- ½ to 1 cup chopped pecans
- ¾ cup butter, melted
- ⅓ cup sugar
- ¼ cup old-fashioned oats
- 2 tablespoons lemon juice
- ¼ teaspoon ground cinnamon

Combine all ingredients in a slow cooker. Cook on high for 3 hours, stirring occasionally. Serve warm with yogurt, waffles or pancakes.

YIELD: 4-6 SERVINGS.

Rosemary Franta, New Ulm, Minnesota

I've handed out this recipe to more people than any other. It has a delicious nutty flavor. It's a light dessert served with plain or vanilla yogurt and can also be a fun brunch treat over pancakes or waffles.

apple granola dessert

COOK TIME: 6 TO 8 HOURS

  4 medium tart apples, peeled and sliced

  2 cups granola cereal with fruit and nuts

  ¼ cup honey

  2 tablespoons butter, melted

  1 teaspoon ground cinnamon

  ½ teaspoon ground nutmeg

Vanilla ice cream *or* whipped topping, optional

In a slow cooker, combine apples and cereal. In a bowl, combine honey, butter, cinnamon and nutmeg; pour over apple mixture and mix well. Cover and cook on low for 6-8 hours. Serve with ice cream or whipped topping if desired.

YIELD: 4-6 SERVINGS.

Janis Lawrence, Childress, Texas

I would be lost without my slow cooker. Besides using it to prepare our evening meal, I often make desserts in it, including these tender apples, which get a tasty treatment from granola cereal.

slow cooker bread pudding

COOK TIME: 3 HOURS

  8 cups cubed day-old unfrosted cinnamon rolls

  2 cups milk

  4 eggs

  ¼ cup sugar

  ¼ cup butter, melted

  ½ teaspoon vanilla extract

  ¼ teaspoon ground nutmeg

  1 cup raisins

Place cubed cinnamon rolls in a slow cooker. In a mixing bowl, combine the next six ingredients; beat until smooth. Stir in raisins. Pour over cinnamon rolls; stir gently. Cover and cook on low for 3 hours.

YIELD: 6 SERVINGS.

EDITOR'S NOTE: 8 slices of cinnamon or white bread, cut into 1-inch cubes, may be substituted for the cinnamon rolls.

Edna Hoffman, Hebron, Indiana

Use a slow cooker to turn day-old cinnamon rolls into a comforting, old-fashioned dessert. It tastes wonderful topped with lemon or vanilla sauce or whipped cream.

hot caramel apples

COOK TIME: 4 TO 6 HOURS

- 4 large tart apples, cored
- ½ cup apple juice
- 8 tablespoons brown sugar
- 12 red-hot candies
- 4 tablespoons butter
- 8 caramels
- ¼ teaspoon ground cinnamon

Whipped cream, optional

1 Peel about ¾ in. off the top of each apple; place in a slow cooker. Pour juice over apples. Fill the center of each apple with 2 tablespoons of sugar, three red-hots, 1 tablespoon of butter and two caramels. Sprinkle with cinnamon.

2 Cover and cook on low for 4-6 hours or until the apples are tender. Serve immediately with whipped cream if desired.

YIELD: 4 SERVINGS.

Pat Sparks, St. Charles, Missouri

Who ever thinks of making dessert in a slow cooker? I do! This old-time favorite goes together quickly…and it's such a treat to come home to the aroma of cinnamony baked apples just like Mom used to make.

chocolate-raspberry fondue

COOK TIME: SERVE IN SLOW COOKER

- 1 package (14 ounces) caramels
- 2 cups (12 ounces) semisweet chocolate chips
- 1 can (12 ounces) evaporated milk
- ½ cup butter
- ½ cup seedless raspberry jam

Pound cake

Assorted fresh fruit

1 In a large saucepan, combine the first five ingredients. Cook over low heat until caramels, chips and butter are melted, about 15 minutes. Stir until smooth.

2 Transfer to a small slow cooker or fondue pot. Serve warm with pound cake or fruit.

YIELD: 5 CUPS.

Heather Maxwell, Fort Riley, Kansas

You don't need a fancy fondue pot to make this melt-in-your-mouth concoction. I serve the dip in my small slow cooker. Folks love the chocolate-raspberry combination.

alphabetical recipe index

Refer to this index for a complete alphabetical listing of all the recipes in this book.

general recipe index

This handy index lists every recipe by food category and/or major ingredient, so you can easily locate recipes to suit your needs.

cook time recipe index

This special index lists every recipe by cook time, so you can quickly find recipes that suit your schedule.

Recipes are listed under the minimum cook time. Many have ranges and may cook longer.